SSAT Mi Level

Prep Book

2023-2024

- 📓 **Note-Taking Techniques:** Discover various methods for taking effective and organized notes during lectures or while reading textbooks.
- 💭 **Critical Thinking Skills:** Develop your ability to analyze, evaluate, and synthesize information to make informed decisions and solve problems.
- ⏰ **Time Blocking and the Pomodoro Technique:** Learn about time management techniques like time blocking and the Pomodoro Technique to enhance productivity
- 🧘 **Stress Relief Strategies:** Overcome exam anxiety with mindfulness, relaxation exercises, and mental resilience techniques.
- 📝 **Practice Makes Perfect:** Explore the importance of practice exams, sample questions, and mock tests, and understand how to analyze your performance to identify areas for improvement.
- 🎯 **Test-Taking Tactics:** Master the art of answering different types of questions, managing your time during the exam, and maintaining focus under pressure.

The following is a disclaimer of liability:

The goal of this book is to provide the reader with background information on the numerous topics that are discussed throughout the book. It is offered for sale with the understanding that neither the author nor the publisher are engaged in the practice of providing professional advice of any type, including but not limited to advice pertaining to legal matters, medical matters, or other matters. In the event that one need the aid of a professional, one must seek the assistance of an experienced professional who is qualified to provide it.

This book has been laboriously labored over in an effort to make it as accurate as is humanly feasible, and it has taken a lot of labor. However, there is a possibility that there are inaccuracies, both in the typography and the actual content of the article. The author and publisher of this book do not accept any responsibility or liability to any third party for any loss or damage caused, or represented to have been caused, directly or indirectly, by the information that is included in this book. This rule applies to any loss or harm that may have been caused, or is suspected of having been caused, by the information that is presented in this book.

This information is provided "as is," without any guarantees or warranties regarding its completeness, accuracy, usefulness, or timeliness. The information is presented "as is" without any guarantees or warranties of any kind. The reader is highly encouraged to seek the opinion of a certified expert or professionals in the field in order to obtain the most up-to-date knowledge that is currently available.

information and compiled data.

In no way, shape, or form does the viewpoints or policies of any specific organisation or professional body come over in this book in any kind whatsoever. Any slights that could be interpreted as being directed toward specific individuals or groups were not intended, despite the fact that they may have occurred.

TABLE OF CONTENT

Before we begin:	7
Understanding the SSAT is covered in Chapter 1.	12
The second chapter is all about getting ready for the SSAT.	22
The Verbal Section is Covered in Chapter 3.	35
Reading Assignments for Chapter 4	46
The Quantitative Section is Covered in Chapter 5.	58
Writing Sample, Section 6, Chapter 6	71
The Chapter 7 Practice Exams are Here!	83
Answers and Explanations are Presented in Chapter 8.	94
The reporting and analysis of scores can be found in Chapter 9.	103
Strategies on the Day of the Test (Chapter 10)	113
Additional Resources is the topic of Chapter 11.	122
Success Stories are covered in Chapter 12.	129
Test Modifications and Accommodations, Chapter 13	137
Techniques for Managing Your Time and Studying Effectively is the Topic of Chapter 14.	145
Dealing with Test Anxiety, which is Chapter 15 of the Book	156
Advanced Math Concepts are Covered in Chapter 16	166
Expanding Your Vocabulary is the Topic of Chapter 17	175
Practice Questions and Answers Explanations 2023-2024	185

STUDY GUIDE

Introduction

Welcome to the SSAT Middle Level Prep Book 2023-2024, your comprehensive guide to acing the Secondary School Admission Test (SSAT) Middle Level! Whether you're a student looking to excel in your SSAT exam or a parent seeking to support your child's educational journey, this book will provide you with the essential knowledge, strategies, and practice materials to succeed.

Chapter 1: Understanding the SSAT

In this chapter, we will introduce you to the SSAT, its importance in the admissions process, and the various levels of the exam. We'll also provide an overview of the test structure, including the types of questions, scoring, and time limits.

Chapter 2: Preparing for the SSAT

This chapter covers the steps you need to take to prepare effectively for the SSAT. It includes advice on setting goals, creating a study plan, and selecting the right materials and resources.

Chapter 3: Verbal Section

The Verbal section of the SSAT assesses your ability to understand and manipulate the English language. We'll delve into the specific question types, provide vocabulary-building tips, and offer practice exercises to sharpen your verbal skills.

Chapter 4: Reading Section

The Reading section measures your comprehension and interpretation skills. This chapter will guide you through reading strategies, approaches to reading passages, and extensive practice exercises.

Chapter 5: Quantitative Section

The Quantitative section evaluates your math skills. We'll cover the math concepts commonly tested, solve sample problems, and explore strategies to improve your performance in this section.

Chapter 6: Writing Sample

The Writing Sample section asks you to respond to a prompt with a well-structured essay. We will provide guidance on organizing your thoughts, creating a compelling argument, and fine-tuning your writing skills.

Chapter 7: Practice Tests

In this chapter, we present full-length SSAT Middle Level practice tests. These tests mirror the actual exam's format and difficulty level, allowing you to assess your progress and identify areas for improvement.

Chapter 8: Answer Key and Explanations

Following the practice tests, we provide detailed answer keys and explanations, helping you understand the reasoning behind each correct answer.

Chapter 9: Score Reporting and Analysis

This chapter explains how the SSAT is scored, when you can expect your scores, and how to interpret them. We'll also discuss the significance of percentiles and what they mean for your admissions prospects.

Chapter 10: Test Day Strategies

Preparation extends beyond content knowledge. We'll offer advice on test-taking strategies, time management, and ways to stay focused and relaxed on the day of your exam.

Chapter 11: Additional Resources

For those looking to further enhance their preparation, we list additional resources, including books, online courses, and tutoring services.

Chapter 12: Success Stories

Read inspiring stories of students who successfully navigated the SSAT journey, from preparation to admissions acceptance, providing you with motivation and real-world examples of what is possible.

Chapter 13: Test Accommodations

This chapter discusses the accommodations available for students with disabilities and how to apply for them. It provides guidance on the documentation required and the process for securing test accommodations.

Chapter 14: Time Management and Study Techniques

Effective time management and study techniques can greatly enhance your preparation. This chapter offers strategies for organizing your study time efficiently and techniques to boost your productivity.

Chapter 15: Dealing with Test Anxiety

Test anxiety is a common issue for many students. This chapter explores practical techniques to manage test anxiety, including relaxation exercises and mindfulness practices.

Chapter 16: Advanced Math Concepts

For students aiming for top scores, this chapter covers more advanced math concepts that may appear on the SSAT Middle Level exam, such as algebra and geometry.

Chapter 17: Vocabulary Expansion
In addition to vocabulary lists, this chapter delves into techniques for expanding your vocabulary in context, making it easier to answer questions in the Verbal section.

Before we begin:

The SSAT Middle Level examination represents a turning point in the lives of numerous students and families at a time when the pursuit of knowledge and personal development is of the utmost importance. This phenomenon occurs within the context of an ever-changing educational landscape. The Secondary School Admission Test, often known as the SSAT, is not only an evaluation of a student's potential to succeed in academics; rather, it is also a portal to a wide variety of educational and personal growth options. In the pages of this comprehensive guide, the SSAT Middle Level Prep Book 2023-2024, we will start on a trip through the complexities of this examination, its repercussions, and the tactics that will empower you to overcome it. This book will be available for purchase in 2023.

Students with varied histories, cultural perspectives, and life experiences sit down to tackle the difficulty of the SSAT Middle Level exam each and every year. If you are a student who aspires to attend a prestigious preparatory school, a parent who is looking for the greatest educational possibilities for your kid, or a teacher who is committed to developing the potential of young minds, the SSAT will play a significant role in your path.

This book has been written with the utmost care with the intention of catering to the requirements of all parties involved in the SSAT process. It is intended to assist students in navigating the complexities of the test, to provide parents with helpful insights and resources, and to act as a resource for instructors who are passionate about enabling students in their pursuit of excellence. The purpose of the website is to aid students through the examination.

In this day and age of ever-increasing rivalry and the pursuit of academic greatness, the SSAT is more than just a test; rather, it is a reflection of the larger philosophical underpinnings of the educational experience as a whole. It tries to grasp the kids' capacity to think critically, to communicate effectively, and to display a level of maturity that is required for overcoming the rigors of a preparatory school curriculum. It does this by going beyond the traditional method of evaluating students' ability to answer multiple-choice questions.

The Importance of the Scholastic Aptitude Test

Before we get into the intricacies of this guide, it is vital that we grasp the significance of the SSAT and why it has acquired its reputation as a critical milestone in the academic journey. This will allow us to get a better understanding of the contents of this guide.

Admissions Catalyst: The SSAT is used by a wide variety of private and independent schools all across the United States and the rest of the world as an essential part of the admissions process. A good number of these institutions have a strong tradition of scholastic distinction and adopt an all-encompassing method of teaching their students. A solid result on the SSAT serves as a critical component of the admissions process, and it has the potential to throw open the doors to a wide variety of educational possibilities.

In addition to assessing a student's academic knowledge, the Scholastic Aptitude Test (SSAT) also serves as a measure of that student's overall aptitude. The purpose of this test is to examine the students' capacity to reason, think critically, and solve issues, all of which are necessary qualities for success in any educational institution as well as in life outside of the classroom.

Students who are preparing for the SSAT are not simply studying for an examination; rather, they are getting themselves ready for the challenges that will be presented to them in the future by way of a rigorous education. They will develop a strong work ethic, resiliency, and tenacity through this process, all of which will serve them well throughout their academic careers and beyond.

Improved Capacity for Communicating Thoughts and Ideas Students take the SSAT Writing Sample portion, which tests their ability to coherently explain their thoughts and ideas. The emphasis placed on effective communication skills is absolutely necessary for academic achievement as well as future success in professional undertakings.

The SSAT is a stepping stone that can lead to a world of academic and personal development. It broadens students' horizons. Students who are able to attend top preparatory schools increase their chances of being exposed to a variety of cultures, ideas, and career paths. This experience has the potential to be formative, contributing to the development of future thought leaders and researchers.

The Road That Lies Ahead

As we move forward through the chapters of this book, you will get familiar with a variety of components that are included on the SSAT Middle Level examination. We will proceed through the Verbal, Reading, and Quantitative parts while providing in-depth insights, test-taking tactics, and practice problems along the way. You will acquire the skills and self-assurance necessary to successfully complete the Writing Sample portion, which will enable you to articulate your ideas in a way that is both clear and precise.

In addition, this book contains practice tests that are similar to the actual SSAT Middle Level exam. These exams will enable you to evaluate your progress and determine the areas in which you need to improve. Understanding the thought process that went into selecting the appropriate answers will be made easier by providing answer keys and explanations in great detail.

In order to ensure that you are well-prepared for the day of the exam, we will go over test-taking strategies, ways for managing time effectively, and techniques for overcoming test anxiety. In addition, we will provide direction on the more general aspects of applying to private schools, such as how to conduct interviews and write application essays.

You will not only unearth a multitude of materials to support your preparation for the SSAT as you make your way through the pages of this book, but you will also acquire vital insights about the SSAT as you make your way through the pages. We want to provide you with the skills necessary to perform well on the 2023-2024 SSAT Middle Level exam and get you started on the road to academic achievement.

The journey for greater knowledge and personal development is a never-ending one, and the SSAT is but one stage along the way in the wider story that is your life. Nevertheless, it is a really significant part of the book, the kind of thing that can direct the course of your study and throw open doors leading to a world of opportunities.

Let us not forget, as we get started on this investigation of the SSAT, that preparation, dedication, and determination are the keys that unlock the doors to opportunity. Your adventure starts here, in the pages of the SSAT Middle Level Prep Book 2023-2024, and it is an honor for us to be your guides as you make your way to the top of the mountain of success.

Disclaimer: The Secondary School Admission Test Board (SSATB) and any other educational institution are not associated with this book in any way, and they have not endorsed or supported it in any way either. It is a self-study guide that was developed to aid students as well as their parents in getting ready for the SSAT.

Understanding the SSAT is covered in Chapter 1.

The Secondary School Admission Test (SSAT) is not merely a test; rather, it is a key that unlocks a world of educational opportunities for students. Your first and most important step toward doing well on this important test is to familiarize yourself with the SSAT. In this chapter, we will look deeper into the relevance of the SSAT, its multiple levels, the test's structure, and scoring, as well as the larger context of the examination in relation to the admissions process for private schools.

The Importance of the Scholastic Aptitude Test

Before we delve into the specifics of the SSAT, it is essential to understand why this test holds as much weight as it does in the context of the educational community. The following essential considerations are necessary to comprehend the significance of the SSAT:

1. An Entrance to Outstanding Educational Opportunities:

Innumerable private and independent schools utilize the SSAT as an essential part of their admissions procedures. These educational institutions are well-known for the rigorous academic standards they uphold, the caliber of their faculty members, and the all-encompassing nature of their curriculum. The Scholastic Assessment Test (SSAT) serves as a key that can be used to open the door to educational excellence for students who are interested in gaining admission to these institutions. A successful performance on the SSAT can throw open a wide variety of doors and possibilities.

2. The Evaluation of Capabilities:

The SSAT is not only an exercise in fact and figure recitation like other standardized tests. The aptitude of a student will be determined by the results of this test. The objective of the test is to determine whether or not the student is able to reason, think critically, and find solutions to issues. These are the kinds of abilities that are necessary not only for academic achievement but also for success in life outside of the classroom.

3. Getting Ready for the Strenuous Work:

There is more to getting ready for the SSAT than just studying for a test. Students will have the chance to practice and get ready for the difficult tasks that will be required of them in their schooling. The activity is beneficial for developing resiliency, tenacity, and a solid work ethic. The abilities that students hone during their preparation for the SSAT will serve them well throughout their academic pursuits as well as their future professional ventures.

4. A Concentration on Interpersonal Communication:

Students will need to be able to properly explain their thoughts and ideas in order to do well on the SSAT Writing Sample part. The emphasis placed on effective communication skills is absolutely necessary for academic achievement as well as future success in professional undertakings. Both educational institutions and potential companies place a premium on candidates who have a solid grasp of the language and the ability to express themselves articulately.

5. Expanding One's Perspectives:

A successful performance on the SSAT is required to gain admission to top preparatory institutions. These schools typically have a wide variety of students and are known for their high academic standards; as a result, they offer a robust educational environment. The transformational power of being exposed to a wide range of cultures, ideas, and chances can help create the future scholars and thought leaders of the world.

In conclusion, the SSAT is much more than a simple standardized test; rather, it serves as a portal to both academic and personal development. It provides students with a one-of-a-kind opportunity to test themselves, perfect their skills, and gain access to educational possibilities that otherwise may not have been available to them.

The several levels of the SSAT

There are multiple tiers of the SSAT, and each one is designed to correspond to a distinct point in a student's progression through their educational experience. The following is a list of the levels:

1. The Elementary Level, sometimes known as EL:

Students who are currently enrolled in grades 3-4 and will be applying to continue their education in grades 4-5 will take the Elementary Level SSAT. At this stage, kids are given their first taste of the testing process and are evaluated on their fundamental abilities in reading, writing, and mathematics.

2. Middle Level, often known as ML:

Students currently enrolled in grades 5-7 who wish to continue their education and move on to grades 6-8 are the target audience for the Middle Level SSAT. It contains parts that evaluate verbal, reading, mathematical, and writing skills respectively.

3. Upper Level, often known as UL:

Students in grades 8 through 11 who are looking to continue their education and enroll in classes 9 through 12 are the target audience for the Upper Level SSAT. At this level, your abilities in reading, writing, mathematics, and verbal communication are put to the test. Additionally, it is a more difficult test than the Middle Level SSAT.

This book's principal concentration is on the Middle Level SSAT since it is designed to meet the needs of a sizeable proportion of students who are getting ready to take the exam. However, a significant number of the tactics and ideas that have been covered in this article can also be used for the Upper Level SSAT if students and parents believe that they will be beneficial for that level of the exam.

The Organization of the SSAT Exam

It is absolutely necessary for successful preparation to have a solid understanding of the format of the SSAT. It gives you the ability to adjust your study strategy to the specific parts of the exam and to strategically use your time and resources. The following are the four primary components that make up the SSAT Middle Level:

1. Description in Words:

Your vocabulary and your capacity to comprehend the meanings of words, their relationships, and their synonyms will be evaluated during the Verbal portion of the test. Questions along the lines of synonym and analogy questions are included.

2. The Reading Assignment:

Your capacity to comprehend and critically evaluate textual texts will be evaluated in the Reading part. Your comprehension of the passages will be evaluated based on how well you can identify the key concepts, describe the details, and explain the author's intent.

3. Discussion of Quantitative Aspects:

Your mathematical prowess will be evaluated in the Quantitative component of the test. You'll need to be able to solve mathematical problems, apply concepts from algebra and geometry, and demonstrate mathematical reasoning to pass this section of the test.

4. A Sample of Your Writing:

The Writing Sample area stands out from the rest of the components in this application. It will give you a question, and then it will ask you to respond to it by writing an essay that is imaginative but also well-structured. The purpose of this section is to evaluate your capacity to communicate clearly through the written word.

The SSAT Middle Level is a test that is completed on paper. You will be given a specific amount of time to finish each component, and the overall length of time that you will have to complete the test will vary based on the level. The entire testing duration for the Middle Level is approximately three hours and five minutes. This time includes any breaks and any instructions that may be given.

The SSAT Scoring Process

It is extremely important to have a solid understanding of the scoring system for the SSAT since this gives you a glimpse into the manner in which the admissions offices of the schools to which you are applying will evaluate your performance. The following is an outline of some of the most important aspects of the SSAT scoring system:

1. The Uncooked Count:

Your raw score is determined by the number of questions for which you answered correctly across all of the test's domains. You will receive one point for every accurate answer, and there will be no deductions for any erroneous responses.

2. Points on a Scale:

The raw values are transformed into scaled scores, which are then used to compare your capabilities to those of other people. It is feasible to compare the scores of students who took several versions of the test thanks to the use of scaled scores.

3. Position in the Percentile:

Your score will be compared to the scores of other students who have taken the SSAT and will be given a percentile rank based on this comparison. If your percentile rank is 85, for instance, this indicates that you performed better on the exam than 85 percent of the other students who took it.

4. Position within the National Percentile:

Your performance is compared to that of students who have taken the SSAT across the country within the last three years using the national percentile rank. It places your scores in a more comprehensive perspective.

5. An Explanatory Report Including:

The interpretative report offers a thorough evaluation of your performance, detailing both the areas in which you excel and those in which you may stand to make some advancements. It is an invaluable resource for making sense of your scores and organizing your path through your academic career.

6. Underscoring:

The Scholastic Assessment Test (SSAT) provides separate scores for the individual sections of the quantitative, verbal, and reading portions of the exam in addition to the total result. Your overall performance in each of these categories is broken down further and more specifically in the subscores.

It is essential to keep in mind that although your scores on the SSAT make up a significant portion of your application, they are not the only element that will be considered in the admissions process. The schools look at your scores with other components of your application, such as your academic records, letters of recommendation, and interviews.

The Situation in Which the SSAT Is Placed

The Secondary School Admission Test (SSAT) is an essential part of the application process for private schools. The educational experiences provided by private schools are typically rather distinctive and significantly distinct from those provided by public schools. When beginning the process of preparing for the SSAT and choosing a school, it is crucial for both students and their parents to have a solid understanding of this broader environment.

The Philosophy of Private Schools:

The way in which students are instructed and educated is frequently guided by the educational philosophies that are used in private schools. For instance, while some institutions place an emphasis on learning through hands-on experience, others place a greater emphasis on academic rigor in the classic sense. You can better align your aims and ideals with the institutions to which you apply if you have a solid understanding of the philosophies held by each institution.

Class Sizes and the Ratio of Teachers to Students:

When compared to public schools, private schools often feature fewer students in each class, as well as a lesser ratio of teachers to pupils. Because of this, students are able to receive more individualized attention and benefit from a more intimate learning atmosphere. It is essential to give some thought to the extent to which these aspects correspond with your individual learning preferences and requirements.

Activities Outside of the Classroom:

The extracurricular offerings at private schools are typically rather diverse, ranging from athletics and the arts to clubs and volunteer opportunities in the local community. Think about the things that are essential to you and how they connect to the things that you're interested in and passionate about.

Community and Cultural Expression:

Every each private school has its own distinct community and culture. It is essential to conduct research on schools and to visit them in order to gain a sense of the culture, values, and diversity that exist within the school community.

Criteria for Acceptance Include:

Scores on the Scholastic Aptitude Test (SSAT) are just one factor that private schools evaluate when making admissions decisions. Other factors include academic records, recommendations from teachers, interviews, and essays. You can improve the strength of your application by gaining an understanding of the holistic approach taken to admissions.

When seen in this broader context, the SSAT functions as a tool of assessing whether or not you are prepared for the academic opportunities and challenges that private schools provide. Your result on the SSAT is evidence of both your academic prowess and your capacity to thrive in the specialized learning environment that these schools offer.

The second chapter is all about getting ready for the SSAT.

When it comes to the Secondary School Admission Test (SSAT), preparation is absolutely essential. This is not an exception to the rule. In this chapter, we will discuss the critical measures that must be taken in order for you to be adequately prepared for the SSAT Middle Level examination that will be given in 2023-2024. This chapter will offer you with a road map to effective SSAT preparation by guiding you through the process of goal formulation, the creation of a study plan, and the selection of the appropriate materials.

Establishing Tangible Objectives

It is essential to define your objectives in a way that is both obvious and attainable before beginning your path of SSAT preparation. Your objectives must to be particular, measurable, and in accordance with your long-term objectives. When determining your goals for SSAT preparation, here are some important things to keep in mind:

1. The Schools in Question:

Think about the institutions that you intend to submit applications to. Do some research on their admission standards, particularly the ranges of acceptable SSAT scores. Your objective should be to earn grades that place you among the top candidates for admission at the schools that you have chosen.

2. Doing Your Own Evaluation:

Consider both the positive and negative aspects of your current academic standing. Determine the areas in which you are weakest and create a goal-oriented study plan for each of the four subtests that make up the SSAT: verbal, reading, math, and writing.

3. A Timeline for the Study:

Find out how many weeks or months are left till the exam you have signed up for. You should set a time limit for each of your goals, and you should devise a study routine that will enable you to go over all of the necessary information in time for the exam.

4. Progress Made in Small Steps:

Create short-term objectives that are attainable and that you can monitor on a regular basis. For instance, you may make it a goal to acquire a specific amount of new vocabulary terms per week or to finish a set of practice questions.

5. Observation and Course Correction:

Check in with yourself on a regular basis to evaluate how far you've come. If you discover that you are slipping behind, you should be ready to make adjustments to your study strategy in order to catch up.

Making a Study Schedule and Plan

Create a detailed study plan as the following stage, keeping in mind the goals you have set for yourself. In order to efficiently prepare, having a strategy that is well-structured is really necessary. The following is an in-depth walkthrough of the process of developing a study plan for the SSAT:

1. Determine the Amount of Free Time:

Figure out how many days or weeks you have left till the SSAT. Be honest with yourself about how much time you can devote to studying every day.

2. Make the Most of Your Time:

Set aside sufficient time to complete each component of the SSAT, including the Verbal, Reading, Math, and Writing sections. Think about your best qualities as well as your areas of greatest improvement, and focus more of your energy on those areas.

3. Decide Which Materials to Study:

Choose the study materials that are in line with the study schedule you created. Books, online seminars, and practice exams for the SSAT are examples of possible preparation materials.

4. Make a timetable for your studies:

Make a study calendar for the week that outlines what you will focus on each individual day of the week. Include a variety of different types of review, such as topic recap, practice problems, and whole mock exams.

5. Establish Important Markers:

In your plan for studying, include specific benchmarks. For instance, you could set a goal to finish a predetermined quantity of practice exams or to complete a predetermined quantity of topic study sections by a predetermined date.

6. Include Rest Periods:

It is necessary to incorporate breaks into the strategy you have for studying. Taking breaks at regular intervals protects your brain from becoming overworked and enables it to process information more efficiently.

7. Remain Faithful to Your Timetable:

Make a pact with yourself to stick to your study schedule. Maintaining a consistent approach is essential for effective preparation.

8. Keep Tabs on Your Advancement:

Take regular practice exams and carefully evaluate how well you did on each one. This should be done on a regular basis. Make use of this knowledge to modify your study plan according to the requirements of the situation.

Choosing the Appropriate Components, Assets, and Resources

One of the most important aspects of getting ready for the SSAT is making sure you have all of the appropriate study tools and resources. When choosing your study resources, the following are some important things to keep in mind:

1. The Official SSAT Study Materials, Including:

The official website for the SSAT offers official study aids in addition to practice exams. These resources are an excellent resource for preparation as they were developed to have a format that is quite similar to the actual SSAT.

2. Study Guides for the SAT:

Numerous preparation books for the SSAT are made accessible by a variety of publishers. You should look for publications that provide a thorough review of the material that will be on the test, as well as practice problems and strategies for taking the test.

3. Les cours en ligne :

Interactive and individualized training can be found in online courses. They often consist of video courses, practice quizzes, and individual commentary on your performance.

4. Services of a Tutoring Nature:

Individualized, one-on-one teaching that is catered to your particular need can be provided by a tutor. Tutors are able to provide specialized assistance in the subject areas in which their students suffer.

5. Sample Exams to Take:

The preparation process should definitely include some practice tests. The more practice tests you take, the more familiar you will become with the layout of the real test as well as the different kinds of questions that will be on it.

6. Resources for Expanding Your Vocabulary:

The development of a robust vocabulary is absolutely necessary for achieving success on the Verbal part. Think about using vocabulary apps, flashcards, or publications that are specifically geared toward expanding your vocabulary.

7. Style Guides for Writers:

In order to complete the Writing Sample portion, you might find it helpful to consult writing manuals or other resources on how to write an effective essay.

8. Discussion Groups and Communities Found Online:

Participating in online discussion groups and communities, such as those found on social media or on websites devoted specifically to SSAT preparation, can be an excellent way to discuss test-taking techniques, share tactics, and learn from the experiences of other students.

9. Tools for Managing One's Time

You can better control your time spent studying with the assistance of tools like timers and apps specifically designed for that purpose.

10. Diagnostic Procedures and Tests

Think about getting a diagnostic exam out of the way before you start your preparation. Your strengths and weaknesses can be identified with the use of a diagnostic exam, which will enable you to create a study strategy that is suited to your specific needs.

11. Accurate Simulations of Actual Exams:

You should make sure that the practice exams you utilize are true to life and appropriately reflect the structure as well as the level of difficulty of the genuine SSAT.

12. Keys to the Correct Answers and Explanations:

You should always be provided with an answer key and explanations alongside your practice tests so that you can fully comprehend the correct answers and the logic that underpins them.

13. Rubrics for Evaluating Essays:

In the section titled "Writing Sample," seek for scoring guides that will explain to you what qualities a good essay should have in order to earn a high mark from the evaluators.

14. Tutoring and Study Groups:

The formation of a study group or participation in an existing one can be an efficient approach to interact with classmates on academic projects and share study tactics and resources.

Keep in mind that the usefulness of your study resources is directly proportional to how well they connect with the objectives and strategies outlined in your study plan. Spend some time doing research and picking out the resources that are going to best serve your preferences and requirements for learning.

The Importance of Taking Practice Exams

Your preparation for the SSAT would not be complete without practice tests. They accomplish a variety of crucial goals, including the following:

1. Become accustomed to:

By taking practice tests, you will become familiar with the layout and organization of the SSAT. You will become more familiar with the test's format as well as the different types of questions if you take many practice exams.

2. Effective Management of Time:

You can improve your ability to manage your time efficiently by taking practice examinations. They provide you with the opportunity to gain a feel for how you should pace yourself throughout the actual examination.

3. The Detection and Analysis of Weaknesses:

You can better understand your capabilities and limitations in each domain by taking practice examinations. You will be able to concentrate on the aspects of your performance that want enhancement if you conduct a performance analysis.

4. Implementation of the Strategies:

The application of test-taking tactics can be facilitated through the use of practice tests. You have the ability to try out a variety of techniques, and then adjust your approach in accordance with the outcomes of those experiments.

5. The Promotion of Confidence:

Your confidence might be boosted if you consistently perform well in practice exams. On the day of the test, it is critical to experience feelings of being prepared and capable.

When taking practice exams, try to recreate the actual examination environment as accurately as you can. Set a timer for yourself, get rid of any distractions, and make the surroundings as calm and focused as possible.

Striking a Balance Between School and Life

A balanced approach is necessary for successful SSAT preparation. Although devoting time to learning is essential, it is as essential to strike a healthy balance between one's professional and personal responsibilities. The following are some approaches that can be taken to achieve this equilibrium:

1. Effective Management of Time:

If you are able to manage your time well, you will be able to achieve your academic goals without compromising on other elements of your life that are equally important. Make a study schedule that fits in with your everyday duties and the activities you normally do.

2. Establishing Priorities:

Determine what your top priorities are. Even while studying for the SSAT is essential, you shouldn't let it get in the way of your entire health and wellness. Make sure you have time for your family, for relaxing, and for your own interests.

3. Relaxation and Time to Unwind:

A good night's sleep and some time to relax are both necessary for efficient learning. Make sure that you get adequate rest so that you can maintain mental clarity and concentration.

4. Engaging in Physical Activity

Your general health and well-being can benefit from engaging in regular physical activity, which can also help reduce stress. In order to maintain your level of energy throughout the day, you need make time for regular exercise.

5. Eating in a Healthy Manner:

Improved focus and cognitive performance are both associated with eating a diet that is nutritionally complete. Consume meals rich in nutrients to enhance the performance of your brain.

6. Support from Social Groups:

Discuss your objectives with your loved ones and close friends so that they can offer you their encouragement and assistance. It can be good to talk about your progress as well as the challenges you face.

7. Methods for Managing Stress:

Maintaining mental composure and clarity requires regular use of techniques for stress management, such as slow, deep breathing, meditation, or mindfulness.

8. the ability to adapt:

Prepare for the SSAT while maintaining some degree of adaptability. Make adjustments to your routine as required in order to account for unanticipated occurrences or personal obligations.

The Verbal Section is Covered in Chapter 3.

The Verbal portion of the Secondary School Admission Test (SSAT) requires students to demonstrate their vocabulary skills as well as their ability to interpret and utilize the English language. This component also pushes students to display critical thinking skills. To do well in this section, you need to know more than simply a bunch of words by heart; you also need to be familiar with the connections between words, the importance of context, and the subtleties of language. In this chapter, we will get into the intricacies of the Verbal section of the SSAT, reviewing the types of questions you may expect to see, tactics for expanding your vocabulary, and methods for efficiently addressing this portion of the test.

What Should Be Expected of the Verbal Part

The purpose of the Verbal portion of the SSAT is to evaluate a candidate's capacity to work with words, comprehend the meanings of those words, and perceive the connections between different words. This section serves a dual purpose, which are as follows:

1. An Evaluation of Your Vocabulary:

Your vocabulary will be evaluated as one of the key focuses of the verbal portion of the test. When it comes to successful communication and comprehension, having a robust vocabulary is really necessary. Your vocabulary will be evaluated on the SSAT by means of questions in which you will be required to choose synonyms and analogies.

2. The Connections Between the Words:

Your ability to recognize connections between concepts will also be evaluated during the verbal portion of the test. This ability goes beyond simply having a large vocabulary and dives into the comprehension of how the meanings of words are connected to one another.

A solid performance in the Verbal part attests to your linguistic abilities and proves that you are academically prepared for the challenges posed by the SSAT as well as the private schools that you hope to attend in the future.

Different Categories of Verbal Inquiry Questions

The Synonym and Analogy questions that make up the SSAT's Verbal part are the test's two primary types of questions in that section. Let's take a closer look at each of these different kinds of questions:

1. Questions Regarding Synonyms

Questions regarding synonyms Your vocabulary will be evaluated by providing you with a focus word and five possible responses to that term. Your job is to pick the word whose meaning is most similar to the one being sought after (the target word).

Take, for instance:

Word of the Day: enormously

Choose an answer: (A) minuscule (B) substantial (C) peculiar (D) extensive (E) insignificant

Extensive is a word that may be used interchangeably with gigantic, so it is the option that should be chosen as the correct response here.

2. Questions of an Analogical Nature:

Your ability to discern relationships between different words will be tested using analogy questions. When you are asked questions based on analogies, you will be given a pair of words that are related in some way. Your mission is to select, from a list of possible answers, a pair of words that correspond to one another in terms of the relationship they have.

Take, for instance:

Example of a Comparative Analogy: A cat is to a feline what a dog is to a.

The options for the answer are as follows: (A) Elephant (B) Lion (C) Canine (D) Fish (E) Bird

Canine is the option that should be chosen as the proper response in this scenario since it has the same relationship as "cat is to feline."

Strategies for the Verbal Section

If you want to do well on the Verbal portion of the SSAT, you need a technique that goes beyond simple memorization and is more deliberate. The following is a list of methods that will assist you in achieving success in this section:

1. Improve Your Language Skills:

In the verbal portion of the test, your most effective tool will be a robust vocabulary. Read a wide variety of books, challenge yourself intellectually, and actively seek to expand your vocabulary. Utilize tools such as flashcards, books, or applications that can assist in expanding your vocabulary.

2. Have a firm grasp of the context:

Be conscious of the fact that the meanings of words are frequently determined by the context in which they are employed. Pay close attention to the ways in which phrases and sections make use of words. This setting can offer hints on the meanings of terms that are unknown to you.

3. Prefixes and Suffixes: a Brief Overview

It is important to become familiar with common prefixes and suffixes since they can provide important clues about the meanings of words. For instance, the prefix "un-" is frequently used to imply negation (for instance, the word "unhappy" meaning "not happy"), while the suffix "-ology" is used to signify an area of study (for instance, the study of life is "biology").

4. Words With Their Roots

Acquire a working knowledge of the foundational words that lie at the heart of the English language. For instance, the prefix "bene-" denotes "good," as seen in terms such as "beneficial" (which is advantageous for you) and "benevolent" (which is kind and good).

5. Make Use of Words Within Their Context:

Make an effort to incorporate newly acquired vocabulary into the speech and writing you do on a daily basis. When you use words in their appropriate contexts, you will find it easier to retain and comprehend the meanings of those terms.

6. Clues from the Context:

When answering questions on synonyms, it is important to pay attention to the context cues provided in the sentence. There are situations when the structure of the sentence or the words that surround the target word can provide signals regarding the meaning of the term.

7. Determine the Connections Between the Words:

When answering questions requiring analogies, you should concentrate on gaining a knowledge of the connections between the various words. Synonyms, antonyms, part-whole, cause-and-effect, and other types of linkages are examples of common types of connections.

8. Put in as much time and effort as possible:

Improving your linguistic skills requires consistent practice, which is absolutely necessary. Participate in a number of different exercises including synonyms and analogies so that you may become familiar with the various word relationships and nuances.

Workouts For The Verbal Portion Of The Exam

Let's put what we've learned about techniques and concepts in the previous section into practice by working through some practice activities. Put your knowledge to the test by answering the following questions:

Exercises in the Use of Synonyms:

Word of the Day: Think About It

Consider (A), Ignore (B), Interrupt (C), Conclude (D), or Encounter (E) Are Your Choices for the Right Answer?

Which of these options for a response can also be described as "ponder"?

Consider is the correct answer for (A).

The Practice of Analogy Questions:

Fill in the blanks of the analogy:

What cold is to something, warm is to something else entirely.

Choose one of these answers: (A) cold (B) icy (C) coolness (D) freezing (E) warmth

Which word best completes the analogy, and how are the two terms connected to one another?

Freezing is the correct answer.

Relationship: The connection between the two parties is very strong. The intensity of "warm" is lower than that of "hot," while the intensity of "cold" is lower than that of "freezing."

Common Mistakes Made in the Verbal Section

Examinees frequently run into the same mistakes on the SSAT's Verbal portion because it is one of the more difficult parts of the exam. A better performance on the day of the test is possible if you are aware of how to avoid the following pitfalls:

1. Response Options That Are Misleading:

In questions requiring you to identify synonyms and analogies, you should exercise caution around response choices that might appear appropriate but do not actually correspond to the intended meaning or relationship of the target words. Always carefully consider all of the available options before deciding which one to pick.

2. Inadequate Vocabulary:

Do not get anxious if you hear or see words that you are not familiar with when you are taking the test. Make educated judgments about their meanings by utilizing the clues provided by the context, as well as your knowledge of prefixes, suffixes, and root words.

3. thinking too much:

While it is necessary to engage in critical thinking, doing so to an excessive degree can cause you to question the veracity of your responses. Have faith in your previous experiences and the skills you've acquired.

4. Effective Management of Time:

Because there is a time limit on the spoken segment, you need to manage your time effectively. Take care not to focus an excessive amount of attention on a single query. Mark the question for further consideration and go on to the next one to ensure that the section is finished in its entirety.

5. Insufficient Context:

When answering questions on synonyms, it is important not to rely solely on your understanding of specific words; rather, you should take into account the context in which the word is used in the phrase.

6. learning by rote without an understanding of the material:

It might be unproductive to memorize word lists without first gaining a knowledge of the words' meanings and the connections between them. Make it a goal to understand the intricacies of the language.

How to Get Your Score in the Verbal Section

It is essential to your ability to interpret your performance on the SSAT that you have a solid understanding of how the Verbal part is graded. The following is critical information regarding the scoring of the Verbal section:

1. The Uncooked Count:

The amount of questions that you got right determines your "raw score" for the "Verbal" part. Because there is no consequence for giving the wrong response, it is in your best advantage to respond to every question, even if you do not know the answer.

2. Points on a Scale:

The unscaled score is then transformed into a scaled score. This scaled score will be used to compare how well you did on the SSAT to the performance of other test takers who have taken different versions of the exam.

3. Position in the Percentile:

Your performance on the SSAT is compared to that of other students who took the test and is shown by your percentile rank. If your percentile rank is 75, for instance, this indicates that you scored higher than 75% of the people who took the test.

4. Position within the National Percentile:

The national percentile rank places your scores within a broader context by comparing them to those of students who have taken the SSAT at the national level over the course of the past three years.

5. An Explanatory Report Including:

The interpretive report offers a thorough analysis of your performance, outlining both the areas in which you excel and those in which you may need some work. It is an invaluable resource for making sense of your scores and organizing your study time effectively.

Reading Assignments for Chapter 4

The Secondary School Admission Test (SSAT) Reading portion requires pupils to demonstrate their comprehension as well as their ability to analyze critically. To do well in this area, you need to be able to do more than just read the passages provided; you also need to be able to comprehend, analyze, and interpret the material. In this chapter, we will go into the specifics of the Reading section of the SSAT, reviewing the types of passages you will face, tactics for effective reading comprehension, as well as approaches for conquering this portion of the exam.

What Should You Expect From the Reading Section

The Reading component of the SSAT is important for evaluating your readiness for a variety of academic tasks since it serves multiple functions. It assesses your capability in the following areas:

1. Read and Understand Texts:

This section is designed to evaluate your reading comprehension abilities, which are absolutely necessary for academic achievement. It evaluates your reading comprehension and determines how well you can decipher textual information.

2. Perform a Textual Analysis:

Your capability to analyze and interpret texts will be evaluated based on the Reading section. Having this ability is essential for comprehending difficult topics and drawing logical conclusions from the information that is provided.

3. Analyze and Evaluate the Arguments:

You will be graded on your ability to analyze the persuasiveness and correctness of the arguments offered in the passages. This skill is necessary for both critical thinking and decision-making, both of which are crucial to modern life.

4. Combine the Accumulated Information:

In this part, your ability to develop an integrated understanding of a subject or problem by drawing together disparate pieces of information from a variety of sources will be evaluated.

The SSAT Reading portion is a key component of the exam since it gives admissions officers insights into your reading and analytical ability, both of which are essential for succeeding in the academic setting of a private school.

The Various Forms That Reading Section Passages Can Take

The Reading component of the SSAT is comprised of four different types of passages that span a wide variety of subject matters and approaches to writing. It is absolutely necessary for efficient preparation to have a solid understanding of the content of these sections. The following are the four sorts of passages:

1. Fiction from the Literary Canon:

The majority of the time, literary fiction passages are taken from longer works of fiction such as novels or short tales. These sections might contain features like as character development, the progression of the plot, or a particular style of narration. To achieve success in literary fiction passages, it is often necessary to have a solid comprehension of the more profound issues and literary techniques that the author employs.

2. The study of social studies:

The subjects of history, culture, society, and politics are frequently the focal points of social studies readings and discussions. There is a possibility that you will come across passages taken from historical records, speeches, or articles that examine events and issues in society.

3. Scientific:

The majority of the time, science sections are made up of factual information and may go into subjects such as biology, chemistry, physics, or environmental science. Your ability to understand scientific concepts and the ramifications of those concepts is essential to your performance on science passages.

4. Arts and Humanities

The topics of philosophy, art, music, and literature are some of the topics that are covered in humanities readings. There is a possibility that you will come across snippets of essays, philosophical literature, or debates of artistic movements.

Techniques for Reading the Sections

In order to do well on the Reading portion of the SSAT, you will need to devise a number of useful techniques for tackling the various kinds of passages that you will be tested on. Consider the following options for your next move:

1. A Quick Look at the Questions:

Take a minute to look over the questions and then read the passage after you've finished. This provides you with an idea of what to look for while reading and helps you keep your attention on the important elements that are being presented.

2. Glance through the passage:

To begin, give the paragraph a cursory read through to obtain a general idea of its organization and content. It is important to pay close attention to the headings, subheadings, as well as the first and last sentences of each paragraph.

3. Participating in the Text:

While you are reading the section, make sure to maintain an active engagement with the text. Notes should be taken, important points should be highlighted, and any portions that stick out or demand additional thought should be highlighted.

4. Determine the Principal Concept:

Find the primary idea or central subject of the passage when you've finished reading it. Accurately answering questions requires first and foremost a comprehension of the core subject matter of the passage.

5. Clues from the Context:

Pay close attention to contextual hints because they may help you understand phrases or ideas that are new to you. There may be explanations or examples provided in the passage that provide light on these phrases.

6. Make a Record of It:

Take notes on important facts, names, dates, and concepts when reading passages related to social studies, science, and the humanities. Because of this, it will be much simpler to respond to particular inquiries.

7. Drawing Conclusions and Using Synthesis:

Get ready to draw conclusions by drawing inferences from the information provided in the passage. It's possible that in order to answer some of the questions, you'll need to combine information from a few different sections of the passage.

8. Don't Make Any Assumptions:

Make sure that your responses are based on the material that is supplied in the text, and not on any assumptions you may have made or any outside knowledge you may have drawn from.

9. Effective Management of Time:

Set a timer for yourself and allot a certain amount of time for each individual paragraph. You shouldn't spend an excessive amount of time on a single section; if you're having trouble understanding it, move on to the next one and come back to it if necessary later.

Reading Section Repetition Drills and Activities

Let's look at a few of different practice activities to show the different concepts and tactics we covered in the previous section. Put your knowledge to the test by answering the following questions:

Exercise in Reading: Fiction from Literature

A Reading Excerpt From:

"Emma cast a quick glimpse at her appearance in the mirror. Her fair skin stood out dramatically against the background of the bright red dress she wore. She had never put on anything quite that vivid in the past. She dithered, pondering whether or not it would be appropriate for her to show up at the party.

The question is:

What is the most important point that the passage makes?

Choices for an Answer:

(A) Emma's musings on the situation

(B) The dress in the color red

(C) Emma's reluctance to take action

(D) The gathering

Answer: (C) Emma's reluctance to answer the question

Exercising the Right to Practice: Science

A Reading Excerpt From:

"In the process known as photosynthesis, plants are able to convert the energy from sunlight into usable chemical compounds. Glucose is the form in which this energy is stored for later use. Plants utilize glucose as a source of energy for growth and reproduction, and it is essential to their survival.

The question is:

According to the passage, what is the most important role that glucose plays in the life of plants?

Choices for an Answer:

(A) So as to absorb the sun's rays

(B) So as to save up some energy

(C) To promote and encourage growth

(D) To ensure that reproduction is possible

Answer: (B) so that energy can be stored

Common Reading: Some Potential Landmines

Students frequently run into typical errors throughout the reading portion of the SSAT, which provides its own unique set of difficulties. The following is a list of typical mistakes that should be avoided at all costs:

1. Hurrying Through the Halls and Passages:

Students may hurry through passages in an effort to save time, and as a result, they miss essential nuances and main themes. You can avoid falling into this trap by dedicating appropriate time to reading and comprehending each passage.

2. Reliance excessively on the Memory:

When responding to questions, students could rely too heavily on their memories, which could result in incorrect responses. Instead of relying on what you remember, you should answer the questions based on the facts offered in the passage.

3. Speculating without the benefit of context:

Some students will just make educated guesses about the meanings of unknown terms or concepts without taking the context into consideration. Before selecting a choice, one should always look for hints from the context.

4. Having second thoughts:

Once you have responded to a question, you should have faith in your judgment and resist the desire to change your response unless there is a significant reason for you to do so.

5. Failing to Understand the Core Concept:

An inaccurate interpretation of the passage's central idea or topic can lead to an improper interpretation of the subsequent questions. Spend some time gaining an understanding of the passage's primary point of concentration.

6. There Is Not Much Time Left:

Ineffective management of time might result in unfinished sections and questions that go unaddressed. During your preparation, give yourself some practice setting a pace that will allow you to answer all of the questions.

Calculating Your Score in the Reading Section

It is essential to your ability to interpret your performance on the SSAT that you have a solid understanding of how the Reading section is graded. The following is important information regarding the Reading section's scoring:

1. The Uncooked Count:

The amount of questions that you answered correctly determines your raw score for the Reading section. Because there is no consequence for giving the wrong response, it is in your best advantage to respond to every question, even if you do not know the answer.

2. Points on a Scale:

The unscaled score is then transformed into a scaled score. This scaled score will be used to compare how well you did on the SSAT to the performance of other test takers who have taken different versions of the exam.

3. Position in the Percentile:

Your performance on the SSAT is compared to that of other students who took the test and is shown by your percentile rank. If your percentile rank is 75, for instance, this indicates that you scored higher than 75% of the people who took the test.

4. Position within the National Percentile:

The national percentile rank places your scores within a broader context by comparing them to those of students who have taken the SSAT at the national level over the course of the past three years.

5. An Explanatory Report Including:

The interpretive report offers a thorough analysis of your performance, outlining both the areas in which you excel and those in which you may need some work. It is an invaluable resource for making sense of your scores and organizing your study time effectively.

The Quantitative Section is Covered in Chapter 5.

The Secondary School Admission Test (SSAT) has a portion called Quantitative that evaluates a student's mathematical ability as well as their ability to solve problems. A strong comprehension of mathematical principles, the ability to apply those concepts to real-world problems, and the capacity to effectively manage one's time are all required for success in this part. In this chapter, we will go into the intricacies of the Quantitative component of the SSAT, covering topics such as the question types that will be asked of you, the techniques that may be used to answer those questions, and the approaches that can be used to effectively tackle this portion of the exam.

What Function Does the Quantitative Part Serve?

When it comes to determining whether or not a student is prepared to tackle difficult academic work, the SSAT's quantitative component plays a number of critical roles in the evaluation process. It determines whether you are able to:

1. Put Mathematical Concepts Into Practice:

In this section, your knowledge of essential mathematical concepts like arithmetic, algebra, geometry, and data analysis will be evaluated.

2. Find Solutions to Problems in the Real World:

You will be given word problems to solve, which will test your ability to apply the mathematical concepts you have learned to real-world scenarios. This ability is necessary for both deliberating and thinking critically about possible options.

3. Conduct a Data Analysis:

Your ability to read and analyze data that is given in the form of graphs, tables, and charts will be evaluated during the quantitative component of the exam. Having this ability is essential in order to arrive at conclusions that are well-informed based on evidence.

4. Be Concerned with the Numbers:

Your ability to work with quantities, comprehend the relationships between them, and produce precise computations will be evaluated.

A student's capacity to deal with the mathematical obstacles that are offered in their curriculum and their readiness for the academic rigor of private schools are revealed by the student's performance well on the quantitative component of the test.

Question Categories Found in the Quantitative Part

In the quantitative portion of the SSAT, there are four primary categories of questions, each of which is designed to examine a different aspect of one's mathematical abilities:

1. Numerical operations:

Questions pertaining to arithmetic center on the four fundamental operations of mathematics: addition and subtraction, multiplication and division, as well as the manipulation of fractions, decimals, and percentages. Calculations and logical reasoning based on numerical data are frequently required to answer these questions.

2. Algebra : [note]

You will be tested on your ability to work with algebraic expressions, equations, and inequalities if you are taking an algebra class. It is possible that you will be asked to solve equations, carry out operations in algebra, or recognize patterns and correlations.

3. Geometry in which:

Your understanding of geometric principles and shape classifications will be tested using geometry problems. Concepts such as angles, triangles, circles, areas, and volumes will come up in the exercises that you are given to complete.

4. Analysis of the Data:

Interpreting the data that is laid out in front of you in tables, graphs, and charts is required for the data analysis problems. Using the material that has been presented to you, you will be required to draw conclusions, evaluate trends, and solve issues.

Strategies for the Quantitative Section

It is not enough to simply memorize formulas if you want to do well on the quantitative portion of the SSAT; you need a strategy that goes beyond that. Consider the following options for your next move:

1. Brush up on the fundamentals of mathematics:

Make sure that you have a solid understanding of the essential ideas of mathematics, such as arithmetic, algebra, and geometry. When necessary, go over some of the most important rules and principles.

2. Become proficient in mental arithmetic:

Work on your mental arithmetic to become more efficient and accurate in your calculations. This information is especially helpful for the problems involving arithmetic.

3. Determine the Most Important Information:

When solving word problems, it is important to recognize both the important information that is supplied and the question that is being asked. To make the issue more manageable, divide it up into smaller pieces.

4. Carry Out Each Step One At A Time:

Find step-by-step solutions to challenges, displaying your effort when it's required. This allows you to keep clarity in your solutions while reducing the likelihood of making errors.

5. Make Use of Other Visual Aids:

When working through problems in geometry, it might be helpful to draw diagrams or make rough sketches of geometric figures. You may find it easier to visualize the issue and come up with a solution if you use visual assistance.

6. Different Methods of Data Analysis:

Exercise your reading and interpretation skills with graphs and tables to prepare for questions on data analysis. Pay close attention to the labels and the units so that there is no room for misunderstanding.

7. Organization of One's Time:

Set aside a particular amount of time to address each inquiry, but avoid concentrating on any one issue for an excessive length of time. Continue on, but be prepared to come back to it if required.

8. Discard the Following Answer Options:

Utilize the process of elimination if you are unsure about the solution to a question. You can improve your odds of picking the right answer by increasing the likelihood that you will cross out response alternatives that are obviously wrong.

Exercises for the Practice of the Quantitative Section

Let's look at some examples of practice problems to see how the principles and tactics we discussed earlier might be put into effect. Put your knowledge to the test by answering the following questions:

Exercise Your Number Skills Question:

The question is:

If a shirt normally sells for $30 but is currently discounted by 20%, what is the price of the shirt after the discount?

Choices for an Answer:

(A) $6

(B) $12

(C) $18

(D) $24

(E) $30

Answer: (C) 18 dollars

Become familiar with algebra Question:

The question is:

Find the value of x by applying the equation: 3x - 5 = 10.

Choices for an Answer:

(A) x = 5

(B) x = 15

(C) x = 7

(D) x = 3

(E) x = 2

Solution: (A) x equals 5

The Following Is a Geometry Practice Question:

The question is:

Find the square's area if each side of the square is 4 inches long; this will give you the square's area.

Choices for an Answer:

(A) 8 centimeters squared

(B) one square foot One square inch

(C) 1 sixteenth of an inch square

(D) twenty-five centimeters square

(E) one quarter of a square foot

(C) 16 square inches is the correct answer.

Analysis of Real-World Data Exercise Question:

The question is:

The amount of books that a class of students read over the course of one academic year is depicted in the graph that can be found below. Which month had the greatest number of books read by the students?

[Insert the bar chart here]

Choices for an Answer:

(A) The month of January.

The month of February

This month is March.

Month of April

(E) May

April is the correct answer.

66

Potential Tripwires in the Quantitative Section

Students frequently run into typical errors while completing the quantitative portion of the SSAT, which poses a unique set of obstacles. The following is a list of typical mistakes that should be avoided at all costs:

1. An Incorrect Understanding of the Questions:

It's possible to give the wrong answer if you don't fully understand the requirements of the inquiry. Carefully read the questions and make sure your answers are addressing the specific concerns raised.

2. A Failure to Pay Adequate Attention to Units:

Pay particular attention to the units of measurement, such as inches, feet, or degrees, when answering questions pertaining to data analysis. If you don't use the right units, you can get the erroneous answers.

3. Trying to Blast Through Difficulties:

Students may rush through difficult problems without completely comprehending them so that they might save time. Before digging into the answer, you should first make sure you fully understand the question.

4. overthinking a situation:

While it is essential to engage in critical thinking, engaging in it to an excessive degree can result in confusion and wrong answers. Keep to the guidelines and standards that you are familiar with.

5. Making mistakes in your calculations:

Calculation errors brought on by carelessness might lead to inaccurate results. Please demonstrate your work in a step-by-step fashion and double check your calculations.

Calculating Your Score on the Quantitative Part

It is essential for interpreting your performance on the SSAT that you have a solid grasp of the grading system for the quantitative part. The following is important information regarding the score of the quantitative section:

1. The Uncooked Count:

The number of questions that you got right determines your raw score for the quantitative portion of the test. Because there is no consequence for giving the wrong response, it is in your best advantage to respond to every question, even if you do not know the answer.

2. Points on a Scale:

The unscaled score is then transformed into a scaled score. This scaled score will be used to compare how well you did on the SSAT to the performance of other test takers who have taken different versions of the exam.

3. Position in the Percentile:

Your performance on the SSAT is compared to that of other students who took the test and is shown by your percentile rank. If your percentile rank is 75, for instance, this indicates that you scored higher than 75% of the people who took the test.

4. Position within the National Percentile:

The national percentile rank places your scores within a broader context by comparing them to those of students who have taken the SSAT at the national level over the course of the past three years.

5. An Explanatory Report Including:

The interpretive report offers a thorough analysis of your performance, outlining both the areas in which you excel and those in which you may need some work. It is an invaluable resource for making sense of your scores and organizing your study time effectively.

Writing Sample, Section 6, Chapter 6

The Secondary School Admission Test (SSAT) includes a portion called the Writing Sample, which gives pupils the opportunity to showcase their creative writing abilities and writing skills. This section is an important component of the examination since it provides admissions officers with information about a candidate's capacity to speak clearly and effectively as well as to articulate their ideas and views. In this chapter, we will discuss the specifics of the Writing Sample section of the SSAT, including the different kinds of prompts that you can be asked to respond to, tactics for producing excellent writing, and approaches to approaching this portion of the exam.

What Exactly Is the Purpose of the Writing Sample?

When evaluating a student's preparedness for the rigors of academic work, the Writing Sample portion of the SSAT serves numerous critical roles, including the following:

1. Evaluation of Your Writing Abilities:

The student's ability to produce clear and logical essays, utilize acceptable language and syntax, and effectively communicate their thoughts is one of the writing skills that are evaluated in this area of the test.

2. Inventiveness and Unpredictability:

Students have the opportunity to demonstrate their creativity and uniqueness in the way that they communicate their ideas and thoughts through the Writing Sample. It inspires students to think critically and to articulate their perspective on whatever subject matter is being discussed.

3. Effective Management of Time:

A student's capacity to compose an essay, organize their thoughts, and finish it within the allotted amount of time is put to the test in this part of the exam because time is a limitation.

4. Capabilities in Communication:

The ability to communicate clearly and concisely is one of the most important skills for academic success. The Writing Sample gives an indication of how well a student can articulate their thoughts and opinions in a way that is both clear and convincing.

Samples of Different Types of Writing Prompts

During the Writing Sample portion of the SSAT, students are often given the option to choose between two different prompts. You are required to choose one of the prompts and respond to it in the form of an essay. The following are some of the categories that the prompts might fit into:

1. Ideas to Prompt Your Creativity:

Students are encouraged to use their imaginations and develop their storytelling abilities via the use of creative prompts. Students are frequently asked to compose either a short story, an imaginative description, or a narrative based on the topic or circumstance that is presented in these prompts.

2. Questions to Prompt Your Own Personal Reflection:

Students are asked to share their views, experiences, or opinions on a particular topic by using personal reflection questions in the classroom. It's possible that these prompts will ask you questions regarding your personal ideals, obstacles, successes, or lessons learned.

3. Prompts for Argumentative and Persuasive Writing:

Students are required to pick a side in a debate and argue why they feel that way by using persuasive prompts, which require them to express their reasoning. In order to support their opinion, they are required to present evidence, examples, and reasoning that is convincing.

4. Prompts for providing Exposition or Information:

Students are asked to explain or describe a topic, concept, or process when they are given expository writing topics. The content that students produce should be understandable, informative, and designed to teach the reader something new.

The particular prompts that students will be given while taking the SSAT may change from one administration of the test to the next. The ability to produce an essay that is both well organized and convincing is essential for success in the Writing Sample, regardless of the prompt that you are given.

Creating Models of Different Strategies

Take into consideration the following methods in order to perform well on the Writing Sample component of the SSAT:

1. Have a Good Understanding of the Prompt:

Before you begin writing, you should make sure you have a thorough understanding of what is being requested of you by thoroughly reading the prompt. Determine the important aspects that are required for each type of prompt, such as creative, personal reflection, persuasive, or expository writing, and list them.

2. Make an Outline for Your Essay:

Spend a moment formulating an outline for your essay. Take into consideration the instances or evidence you wish to provide, as well as your main ideas, the format of your essay (introduction, body paragraphs, conclusion), and the organization of your essay.

3. Arrange Your Thoughts in an Orderly Manner:

In the essay you are writing, express your ideas in a way that is logical and well ordered. Make sure that each paragraph has a distinct purpose and adds something to the broader argument or story that you are telling.

4. Go into Further Detail and Provide Evidence:

When presenting points or arguments, be sure to elaborate on them and provide supporting evidence in the form of instances or evidence. Essays that are very strong typically feature particular instances, data, or personal experiences.

5. Check for errors and make edits:

Make good use of the remaining time by revising and editing your essay. Check not only for faults in grammar and spelling but also for clarity and consistency in the writing. Make certain that your writing can be understood by everybody.

6. Observe the Allowed Time and Word Count:

Maintain adherence to the word count requirement that was specified for your article and time yourself appropriately. Spending an inordinate amount of time planning and writing a single section of your essay should not come at the expense of the other sections of your paper.

Creating Models of Exercises for Practicing

The following are some sample questions and responses to give you an idea of the kinds of writing that may be required of you in the section under Writing Samples:

Inspirational Prompt:

To begin:

Create a piece of flash fiction with the opening line, "It was a dark and stormy night."

Here's an Example Response:

It was a stormy night and the sky was really dark. Rain pounded against the windows as the trees rustled in response to the howling wind. A few members of the household could be seen congregating close to the warm fire in the living room. They had no idea that the stormy night they were experiencing would alter the course of their lives for good.

Prompt for Individual Introspection:

To begin:

Describe a period in your life when you were presented with a problem that appeared impossible to solve. How were you able to get past it, and what did you take away from the experience that it taught you?

Here's an Example Response:

My move to a new school was one of the times in my life that presented me with the greatest amount of difficulty. I had the impression that I didn't belong and was having trouble finding my niche in the group. It appeared to be impossible to satisfy the urge to adjust and find new acquaintances. Having said that, as time went on, I became aware of the significance of perseverance and resilience. I reached out to other people, asked for assistance from my instructors, and eventually got back on my feet. This incident instilled in me the significance of maintaining a positive attitude and requesting assistance whenever I was confronted with a difficult situation.

Argumentative and Persuasive Writing Prompt:

To begin:

Do you think that students should have more time off from school over the summer? Compose an article in which you discuss this subject from the perspective that you take, and provide reasons and evidence to back up your claims.

Here's an Example Response:

The existing length of the summer break that schools enjoy should absolutely not be changed in my opinion. Some people believe that a longer break would lead to increased opportunities for relaxation and pleasure, but the truth is that it can cause students to fall behind in their academic progress. Because of the potential for academic abilities to be lost during an extended hiatus, students who return to school after such a sabbatical may require significant revision. In addition, a prolonged hiatus may cause disruptions in family schedules and make it more difficult for parents to balance the demands of their careers with the obligations of caring for their children.

Prompt for expository or informative writing:

To begin:

Give an explanation of the process of photosynthesis and the role it plays in the survival of plant life. Please provide a description that is both clear and instructive of this crucial step in the biological process.

Here's an Example Response:

The very important biological process known as photosynthesis is the mechanism by which green plants and various other creatures transform the light energy they absorb into the chemical energy known as glucose. This activity, which takes place inside the chloroplasts of plant cells, is absolutely necessary for the continued existence of plant life and all forms of life on earth. During the process of photosynthesis, plants take in carbon dioxide from the surrounding air and use the energy from the sun to transform the carbon dioxide into glucose and oxygen. The glucose provides the plant with a source of energy, which in turn supports the plant's development and reproduction. Meanwhile, the oxygen that is released into the atmosphere has a positive impact on the environment since it helps to refill the atmosphere with air that can be breathed.

Mistakes That Are Usually Made When Writing Examples

In the area of the SSAT called Writing Sample, students have a chance of encountering several typical traps that can have an impact on the quality of their essays. To steer clear of these dangers, keep the following in mind at all times:

1. Responses That Are Off Topic:

It is a common mistake to write a response that either veers off subject or does not precisely address the prompt that was given. Make sure that your essay continues to focus on the subject or topic that has been provided.

2. Insufficient Clarity:

Your essay may be difficult to understand if the writing is unclear or if it is not ordered well. You should use transitions to connect your ideas and organize your thoughts in a logical, sequential order.

3. Incorrect Use of Grammar and Spelling:

Your writing could be considered of lower quality if it had grammatical faults and spelling issues. Correct these errors by reading your essay over again once you've proofread it.

4. Responses that are Way Too General:

It is possible to produce a less appealing essay by providing an answer that is general or ambiguous and lacks specific instances or facts. Give your article more gravitas by referring to specific examples or events from your own life.

5. Irresponsible Essays:

Writing in a hurry and not being able to adequately manage your time can both lead to hasty essays that have little substance. Make effective use of the time you have available, and plan out your essay before you start writing it.

The Evaluation of the Writing Sample

It is essential for analyzing your performance on the SSAT that you have a solid grasp on the grading rubric for the Writing Sample. What follows is essential information regarding the grading of your writing sample:

1. A Holistic Approach to Scoring:

A comprehensive method is often used to determine the score for the Writing Sample. This indicates that the essay is reviewed in its whole, taking into consideration aspects such as the clarity of expression, organization, progression of ideas, and overall effectiveness.

2. The Absence of a Specified Rubric:

The Writing Sample is not graded according to a predetermined rubric or predetermined checklist of requirements. Instead, the essay is graded by qualified raters according to its overall quality, which takes into account the essay's coherence, persuasiveness (if relevant), creativity (if applicable), and clarity (if applicable).

3. The possible range of scores is from 1 to 6:

Words on paper Typical scores vary from one (the lowest) to six (the highest), with one being the lowest and six being the highest. Every essay is graded separately by two different scorers, and the resulting scores are then averaged to obtain a total grade for the essay.

4. There Is No Correct Or Incorrect Answer:

The purpose of the Writing Sample is not to produce a "right" or "wrong" answer, but rather to demonstrate good communication and critical thinking skills.

5. Critical analysis of the content and expression:

The content of the essay, including the ideas, arguments, and examples offered, as well as the expression of those contents, including clarity, language, and style, are both taken into consideration by the graders.

6. Repercussions for Admissions:

Even though it is only one part of the SSAT, the Writing Sample may be given a considerable amount of consideration during the admissions process. It gives admissions examiners a sample of your writing ability and demonstrates that you have the capacity to effectively communicate thoughts in writing.

The Chapter 7 Practice Exams are Here!

Taking some practice tests is an essential part of getting ready for the SSAT. They are useful tools for determining your current level of preparedness, determining your strengths and shortcomings, and boosting your confidence in preparation for the real test. This chapter digs into the value of practice exams, strategies for taking them, and advice for making the most of your preparation by making use of these essential tools.

The Importance of Performing Well on Mock Exams

Your preparation for the SSAT will benefit greatly from taking practice tests for a number of reasons:

1. An Evaluation of Your Present Capabilities:

You can determine how well prepared you are for the various portions of the SSAT, including the Verbal, Reading, Math, and Writing assessments, by taking practice tests. This evaluation will highlight both your areas of strength and those in which you could use some work.

2. Familiarity with the Format of the Examination:

You can become very familiar with the format of the SSAT if you prepare for it by working through some practice tests. You will become familiar with the various types of questions you will be asked, as well as the structure of the examination and the time limits for each segment.

3. Capabilities in Time Management:

You will learn how to appropriately divide up your time across each area by practicing with practice tests. Learning how to manage your time is the only way to guarantee that you will finish every segment within the allotted amount of time.

4. Instilling a Sense of Confidence:

Taking practice exams might help you feel more comfortable in test-taking situations and increase your confidence. When it comes time to take the actual SSAT, you will feel more confident in your abilities as you get more familiar with the test's layout and its subject matter.

5. Identifying Areas That Need Improvement:

Taking practice examinations will help you identify any areas in which you might benefit from additional study time. When you are aware of the areas in which you struggle, you are better able to concentrate your efforts and learn in a more planned manner.

6. Adjustment to the Conditions of the Test:

You can better adapt to the actual testing conditions by practicing under conditions that are similar to those of the test. These conditions include time constraints and a calm location.

Getting the Most Out of Your Practice Exams

Take into consideration the following tactics in order to get the most out of your practice tests:

1. Recreate the Conditions of the Test:

You should take your practice tests in an atmosphere that is designed to replicate the real test. Find a place with less noise, give yourself a time limit, and get rid of any distractions.

2. Analyze and Learn from Your Errors:

After you have finished an exercise test, it is important to carefully go over your answers. Pay particular attention to the questions that you answered poorly or those that were difficult for you to answer. Acknowledging and learning from one's own errors is necessary for personal growth.

3. Conduct an Evaluation of How Time Is Spent:

Evaluate the manner in which you used your time when taking the practice test. Have you allowed yourself insufficient time to complete the other sections because you spent too much time on one? Make the necessary adjustments to your approach for managing your time.

4. Create a Learning Strategy:

Create a study strategy for yourself that zeroes in on your areas of weakness by basing it on how well you did on practice examinations. Give yourself additional time to work on the topics or portions in which you feel you need the most improvement.

5. Test Strategies That Are Replicated:

When you practice for the test, make sure to include the new tactics you've learned. For example, put your tactics for reading comprehension to use in the Reading portion, and put your methods for solving problems to use in the Math section.

6. Participate in a Number of Exams:

You shouldn't put all of your faith into a single mock exam. Take a variety of exams so that you can get a more comprehensive picture of your capabilities and limitations. This wide range of questions on the exam might help you get ready for a variety of different situations.

Utilizing Practice Exams to Get the Most Out of Your Preparation

If you want to maximize the effectiveness of your preparation for the SSAT using practice exams, follow these guidelines:

1. Get an Early Start:

Start preparing for the SSAT by giving yourself practice exams a good long time in advance of the actual examination. You will be able to discover areas in which you need to improve and then modify your study strategy to accommodate these areas if you start early.

2. The Importance of Being Consistent:

Include taking practice exams on a regular basis as part of your study routine. Maintaining consistency across all aspects of your performance allows you to consistently hone your talents and monitor your advancement.

3. A Step-by-Step Incrementation of Difficulty:

Start with practice examinations that are less difficult and work your way up to those that are more difficult as you progress. You will be able to gradually hone your abilities with the help of this development.

4. Recreating the Conditions of the Actual Test:

When taking practice tests, you should adhere to the same time limitations and conditions for testing as you would on the actual SSAT. This prepares you for the environment that you will really be tested in.

5. Go Over Everything Carefully:

After you have finished an exercise to test your knowledge, carefully go over your answers, both the correct ones and the incorrect ones. It is essential to one's growth to have a solid understanding of the logic behind each possible solution.

6. Concentrate on Your Weak Points:

Utilize the outcomes of your practice tests to help you pinpoint your areas of improvement. Devote a greater amount of your study time to these chapters or ideas.

7. Keep Tabs on Your Advancement:

You should maintain a record of your performance as well as the results you receive on your practice tests. Monitoring your advancement can be an effective way to inspire you and provide insight into patterns in your performance.

8. Seek the Advice of Qualified Professionals:

If you are having trouble improving your results, you may think about enrolling in a preparation program for the SSAT or obtaining the assistance of a qualified tutor. They are able to deliver training and tactics that are specifically tailored.

9. Keep a Positive Attitude:

Throughout the entirety of your preparation, remember to keep a good mindset. It is important to not let poor performance on practice examinations discourage you. Keep in mind that the goal of the practice tests is to help you become a better student.

Applying Oneself to the Official SSAT Practice Tests

There is no substitute for taking official SSAT practice tests, which are made available by the SSAT organization. They provide an accurate depiction of the

SSAT, allowing you to practice in settings that are designed to be very similar to the conditions under which you will be taking the exam. The official practice exams are the most accurate kind of test preparation material because they are designed to replicate the structure, subject matter, and level of difficulty of the SSAT.

You can acquire official SSAT practice exams from the SSAT website. These tests are available in a variety of levels that correspond to the SSAT Elementary, Middle, and Upper Levels. If you want your official practice exams to be as helpful as possible, make sure to follow these guidelines:

1. Take the official practice tests only when absolutely necessary:

The official practice tests provide students with the most accurate preview possible of the real SSAT. Make strategic use of them by giving yourself full-length practice examinations at significant junctures in your studying process.

2. Participate in Timed Tests

When using certified practice tests, it is imperative that you stick to the allotted amount of time for each area. Learning how to schedule yourself is an essential part of developing abilities in time management.

3. Go Over Everything Carefully:

After you have completed an official practice exam, you should carefully go over your answers. Learn the reasoning behind why some of the answers are correct while others are incorrect.

4. Educate Yourself from Your Errors:

Create a list of the different categories of questions or topic areas in which you tend to make errors repeatedly. Concentrate on enhancing your abilities in these specific domains.

5. Recreate the Conditions of the Test:

Participate in official practice tests held under conditions that are designed to simulate the SSAT environment. Find a place with little or no background noise, get rid of any potential distractions, and keep a strict timer.

6. Evaluate Your Performance Based on:

Pay close attention to any patterns that emerge in your scores on the official practice tests. It's a good sign of development if you're able to observe consistent gains in your performance. If your scores have not changed, it is time to rethink both your study strategy and the areas in which you are concentrating.

Practice Exams Conducted by a Third Party

In addition to the official SSAT practice tests, you could also come across materials for practice tests provided by third parties. These are potentially helpful additions to your preparation, but you should make sure to use them with care. The following are some things to keep in mind before using practice exams provided by a third party:

1. The Quality of the Content:

Examine the standard of the practice exams provided by other parties. Make sure that the questions are consistent with the content and organization of the SSAT.

2. Being consistent:

There is a possibility that the difficulty level and structure of third-party practice exams will not be the same as those of the official SSAT assessments. Instead of relying on them as your primary source of preparation material, use them as supplemental resources.

3. Maintain a Healthy Relationship with Official Tests:

You should only use practice tests from third parties as a supplement to your preparation and not as a replacement for the official SSAT practice tests. The accuracy of a test's portrayal can be best gauged by taking the official test.

4. Go Over the Answers:

When using practice exams provided by a third party, it is important to go back and look at your answers and learn from your mistakes. Despite the fact that the quality of these tests can range widely, the process of analyzing and growing from mistakes continues to be beneficial.

5. Combine This Information with That of Other Resources:

In order to construct a well-rounded strategy, you should incorporate third-party practice tests into your overall study plan. These tests should be used in conjunction with other SSAT preparation tools, such as study guides, flashcards, and tutoring.

Answers and Explanations are Presented in Chapter 8.

In this section, we will offer you with a key to the answers as well as in-depth explanations for a variety of SSAT practice questions that you have previously worked on. These explanations will help you understand the rationale that went into selecting the correct answers, and they will also provide insight into how you should approach problems of a similar nature on the actual test. Keep in mind that the SSAT is broken up into different levels (Elementary, Middle, and Upper), and the questions that follow are meant to give you an idea of what you might see on the test.

Verbal Constituents:

Let's get started with the Verbal portion, which evaluates your ability to read and comprehend passages as well as your vocabulary.

1. A Question Concerning Synonyms

The question is:

Pick the word that comes closest to describing the sense conveyed by "perplexing."

Choices for an Answer:

(A) Incomprehensible

(B) Uncomplicated

(C) Absolutely delightful

(D) In a relatable way

(E) To an extreme degree

(A) It is difficult to understand.

Detailed explanation:

In the context of describing something that is confused or baffling, the word "perplexing" is frequently employed. "confusing" (option A) is the response choice that most closely corresponds in meaning to "perplexing." The remaining choices do not evoke the same level of confusion or complexity as the first choice.

2. Question Regarding an Analogy:

The question is:

Choose the two words that fit together most naturally to finish the analogy:

In the same way as _____ is to a dog, BARK is to trees.

Choices for an Answer:

(A) Fur

(B) Groan

(C) The choker

(D) Residence

(E) Meowing

Answer: Collar (option C)

Detailed explanation:

The word "BARK" is related to the word "TREE" in the sense that one will often find tree bark on trees. On a related note, a "COLLAR" is something that is frequently seen on a dog. The analogy is not correctly finished using any of the other potential answers.

Reading Part: [Chapter]

Moving on to the Reading component of the SSAT, this portion of the exam evaluates how well you can comprehend and evaluate written texts.

1. Question to Determine Your Level of Reading Comprehension:

A Reading Excerpt From:

An adventurous journey to the South Pole was undertaken by a band of intrepid travelers at the turn of the 20th century. This group, which was led by Sir Ernest Shackleton, was put through unfathomable hardships, including exposure to extreme cold, malnutrition, and solitude.

The question is:

What was the most difficult obstacle that the explorers had to overcome throughout the passage?

Choices for an Answer:

(A) A lack of previous work experience

(B) Very low temperatures

(C) There is a limited amount of food

(D) An excessive amount of apparatus

(E) Regular interaction with other people

Answer: (B) Extremely low temperatures

Detailed explanation:

The difficulty of "extreme cold" is mentioned as one of the difficulties that the explorers had to overcome throughout the journey. Because the reading makes this point very clear, selecting this option as the response is appropriate.

2. Question Drawing an Inference:

A Reading Excerpt From:

"Julia was known to spend the most of her time on the weekends in the community library. She was frequently observed with a pile of books, and the staff at the library was familiar with her by name. Everyone who knew her could clearly see how much she enjoyed reading.

The question is:

From what you've read, what conclusions can you draw about Julia?

Choices for an Answer:

(A) Julia never went to the library on the weekends or on holidays.

(B) Julia never read anything outside of the library.

(C) Reading was not something that Julia enjoyed doing.

(D) Julia was a patron of the library on a consistent basis.

A place of employment for Julia was the library.

(D) Julia was a frequent patron of the library throughout her life.

Detailed explanation:

This chapter details Julia's love of reading as well as her regular trips to the library on the weekends. The fact that you have this knowledge allows you to draw the conclusion that Julia frequented the library and enjoyed reading, hence the answer that you are looking for is (D).

Section on Mathematics:

Now that we've gotten that out of the way, let's move on to the mathematics portion of the test, which evaluates your mathematical skills and your ability to solve problems.

1. A question involving arithmetic

The question is:

What is the remaining quantity of apples if you start with 5 and eat 2 of them?

Choices for an Answer:

(A) 0

(B) 1

(C) 2

(D) 3

(E) 5

3 is the correct answer

Detailed explanation:

If you begin with five apples and eat two of them, you will be left with three apples after performing the math: five minus two equals three.

2. A Question Regarding Geometry:

The question is:

What is the surface area of a square that has sides that are each 4 inches long?

Choices for an Answer:

(A) equal to four square inches

(B) 8 centimeters squared

(C) one square foot One square inch

(D) 1 sixteenth of an inch square

(E) 20 millimeters squared

(D) 16 square inches is the correct answer.

Detailed explanation:

The area of a square can be calculated using the formula: side length multiplied by itself twice. In this instance, the area of 16 square inches is equivalent to the area of 4 inches squared.

This is the writing section.

In the end, let's have a look at an example question from the Writing part and some possible replies.

Prompt for an Example of Writing:

To begin:

Create an essay that discusses the significance of being nice in day-to-day life.

Here's an Example Response:

Kindness is an essential attribute that has a significant impact on the way we conduct our lives on a daily basis. It is the capacity to be sociable, giving, and considerate, and it has the power to cultivate goodwill and develop meaningful connections between persons. Not only is kindness necessary for developing healthy relationships, but it's also important for making the world a more pleasant place to live.

Kindness is essential in day-to-day life for a number of reasons, but one of the most important ones is that it contributes to the development of a sense of community and belonging. When people treat one another with consideration, they provide the groundwork for trust and cooperation. Kind deeds have the power to unite and bring people closer together in settings as diverse as families, workplaces, and communities. These seemingly insignificant actions of generosity, such as lending a hand to a neighbor who is struggling or

flashing a warm smile at a total stranger, assist to create a more harmonious community.

Additionally, the act of kindness has a significant influence on the mental and emotional health of individuals. When we extend our compassion to other people, we bring happiness and fulfillment into our own lives. Endorphins, which are natural mood lifters, are released when good acts are performed. Additionally, acts of kindness have been shown to lower levels of tension and anxiety, both of which contribute to a more happy mental state. Kindness, when used in this way, not only benefits the people who are on the receiving end of it, but also the people who practice it.

The reporting and analysis of scores can be found in Chapter 9.

It is critical for students as well as their parents to have an understanding of how SSAT scores are reported and to be able to interpret those scores. In this chapter, you will gain an understanding of the structure of the SSAT scores, how they are reported, and what they represent for your application to private institutions.

Acquiring Knowledge of the SSAT Score Scales

The SSAT is comprised of multiple levels, and depending on which level you choose to take, the scoring scale will be varied. There is an Elementary Level, a Middle Level, and an Upper Level. The Elementary Level is for students in grades 3-5, the Middle Level is for students in grades 5-7, and the Upper Level is for students in grades 8-11. Every level has its own grading scale, and even within each level, the Verbal, Reading, Quantitative, and Writing parts each have their own score.

1. Sections on Verbal Ability, Reading Comprehension, and Numerical Reasoning:

The Verbal, Reading, and Quantitative parts each have a scoring range that normally falls between 440 and 710 points. The score of 500 is typically chosen to represent the mean or average of these components. The scoring scale is designed to accommodate a distribution of scores, and the percentiles are used to reflect this distribution.

2. The Writing Component:

The Writing portion of the exam receives a different score. A distinct score on a scale ranging from one to six is assigned to it. Two different readers will each give your essay a score out of six on a scale from one to six. These scores will then be averaged together to give your essay a total score between two and twelve. The score of 1 is the worst possible score, and the score of 6 is the best possible score. The score you receive on the Writing portion is not added to the scores you receive on the other SSAT sections; yet, it is an essential component of how well you perform on the exam as a whole.

Ranks according to the percentile system

Your percentile ranks are provided in addition to your SSAT scores. The percentile rank provides an estimate of the proportion of students who performed more poorly than you did on the test. If your percentile rank is 70, for instance, this indicates that you scored higher than 70 percent of the people who took the test. A better performance in comparison to that of other students is reflected by a higher percentile rank, which is considered a positive indicator. Because they put your scores into perspective, the percentile ranks that you earned are of utmost significance to the admissions officers.

Comprehending the Contents of the SSAT Score Report

If you take the SSAT, the following sections will be included in the score report that you receive:

1. Scores for Each Individual Section:

On your score report, your results for the Verbal, Reading, Quantitative, and Writing portions will be displayed, along with their respective percentile ranks. Your score report will also include an overall percentile rank. This breakdown sheds light on the areas in which you excel as well as those in which you struggle.

2. The final tally is:

Your scores from the Verbal, Reading, and Quantitative parts will be added together to determine your overall score. The total is the sum of the scaled scores from each of these sections, and it can range anywhere from 1320 to 2130 points total. The overall score provides a comprehensive summary of how well you performed on the SSAT.

3. Example of Your Writing Score:

Your essay that you write for the Writing portion will receive a different score that is determined by the Writing Sample score. This score, which is based on a scale ranging from 2 to 12, is the cumulative score of two separate readers.

4. Ranks based on the Percentile:

Your score report will have percentile ratings broken down for each category. These ranks provide a context for your scores by displaying how they compare to those of other individuals who took the test. For example, if your percentile rank is 75, it indicates that you scored higher than 75 percent of all students.

5. Reports on the Students' Performance at Their Specific Schools (Optional):

When you registered for the SSAT, you were given the option to pick schools to receive your scores. Those schools will now receive a school-specific score report. This report is intended for admissions offices, and it will generally give extra information, such as a comparison of your score to the pool of applicants that the institution is considering.

The Role That SSAT Scores Play in the Admissions Process

Scores on the SSAT are used in the admissions process of private schools as one of the components. The following is a typical example of how admissions offices make use of SSAT scores:

1. The preliminary screening:

Scores on the SSAT are frequently used as an initial screening technique by admissions personnel. Your application will advance further in the admissions process if the scores you submitted meet the minimum requirements set forth by the school.

2. Preparedness for Academic Success:

Your scores on the SSAT are used by schools to evaluate your level of academic preparedness and your capacity to handle the curriculum. Scores that are higher are typically indicative of an academic background that is robust.

3. Evaluations in Relation to Peers:

The use of percentile ranks enables admissions officers to evaluate a candidate's performance in relation to that of other candidates. They take into account where you stand in comparison to the other contenders.

4. General Observations and Ratings:

Although your SSAT scores are very significant, they are only one component of your application. The admissions committee will also take into account other aspects of the applicant, such as their academic history, recommendations from teachers, interviews, and extracurricular activities.

5. A Sample of Your Writing:

Your writing abilities, which are essential for a wide variety of facets of academic work, can be evaluated with the Writing Sample. The capacity to eloquently and clearly convey ideas is one of the skills that admissions examiners look for in a candidate's writing sample.

6. Minimum Requirement for a Score:

Because the requirements and preferences for scores might vary from school to school, it is necessary to do research on the institutions to which you will be applying and gain an understanding of what is expected of you.

Comparison of Scores and Option to Choose a Score

You have the ability to choose which colleges will be notified of your SSAT scores through a program called "Score Choice," which is offered by the SSAT. If you plan to take the SSAT more than once but only want to give the colleges you're interested in your top score, this feature can be helpful. The following are some important details about Score Choice:

1. Your Selection of a Score Is Voluntary:

The utilization of Score Choice is totally voluntary. Your scores will be sent to all of the schools that you specified when you registered for the SSAT, even if you decide not to use the optional scoring service.

2. Take Into Account the Policies of Each School:

There is a possibility that various schools will have varied policies regarding score choice. While some institutions may be more flexible in their requirements, others may insist on seeing all of your SSAT results. Before determining whether or not to use Score Choice, it is absolutely necessary to check the policies of each institution.

3. Only the Highest Scores Are Considered:

When you choose Score Choice, you will have the ability to choose which of your scores will be sent to the colleges. If you have taken the SSAT more than once, you have the option to send only your greatest results for each part. This might be an advantageous strategy if you have a history of doing well on the test.

4. Fewer Available Options:

You are not permitted to combine or combine randomly selected scores from multiple test dates while using Score Choice. You are required to turn in all of your scores from a single test date for each individual section.

Taking the SSAT all over again

If you feel that your first scores on the SSAT are not representative of your true potential, you should think about retaking the exam. The following are some things to keep in mind:

1. The preparatory work:

Investing time in further preparation is necessary before taking the SSAT again. Determine the parts of the test where you performed poorly and work on getting better in those specific areas.

2. Option for Scoring:

Score Choice allows you to send only your highest results to colleges, which can be helpful if you want to retake the SSAT.

3. Dates for the Examinations:

Because the SSAT is given numerous times throughout the year, you have the flexibility to choose a test day that coincides with the timetable you have set for your preparation.

4. Important Dates for School:

Remember that the application deadlines for private schools must be met. Make it a point to schedule your retake around the application deadlines of the educational institutions that you are interested in attending.

5. Cap the Number of Retakes:

Although taking the SSAT more than once is a possibility, you should try to limit how often you do so. If a candidate has taken the exam an excessive number of times, admissions staff might challenge them. To increase your scores, you should concentrate on targeted preparation.

How to Make Sense of Your Score Report

When you obtain the report of your SSAT scores, it is critical that you interpret the findings in order to comprehend how well you performed. When analyzing your score report, the following are some important considerations to keep in mind:

1. Contrast These Results with the School Averages:

Do some research on the colleges to which you are applying and evaluate how your grades stack up against the typical student's grades there. This might give you an idea of how competitive your application is at each school.

2. Recognize Your Weaknesses:

Analyze your results to see the areas in which you could improve. This might assist you in determining the areas in which you should concentrate your efforts for improvement.

3. Ranks based on the Percentile:

Pay close attention to your percentile rank so that you can determine how well you did relative to the other people who took the test. In most cases, a better position is indicated by a higher percentile rank.

4. A Sample of Your Writing:

Do not undervalue the significance of submitting a Writing Sample. If you submit a weak essay, however, your application can look worse than if you submitted an excellent one.

5. Take into consideration the Overall Score:

Although individual section scores are significant, the overall score offers a more comprehensive evaluation of your work.

6. Policies Regarding Admissions:

Check out the admissions criteria of the colleges and universities to which you are applying. It's possible that certain institutions put more weight on SSAT scores than others, while others take a more well-rounded approach.

Strategies on the Day of the Test (Chapter 10)

The day you take the SSAT is a pivotal point in the admissions process you are going through. This chapter offers in-depth advice on how to approach the day of the exam, covering everything from what to do in the days leading up to the test to suggestions for coping with test-day anxiety and performing to the best of your ability on the actual exam.

Preparation Ahead of the Day of the Exam

Get Plenty of Rest Getting enough sleep is essential for maintaining mental alertness and concentration. Aim to get between seven and nine hours of high-quality sleep per night in the days coming up to the exam.

last Review: During this last review, you should go over any notes, study materials, or practice questions that have been beneficial to you throughout the preparation process. However, you should try to avoid cramming the night before the test because doing so can make your anxiety levels rise.

Prepare Your Test Materials: Ensure That You Have All of the Necessary Items, Including Your Admission Ticket, Identification, Pencils, Erasers, a Calculator (If Allowed), and a Watch to Keep Track of the Time Make Sure You Have All of the Necessary Items Before You Take the Test.

Become Familiar with the area and Plan Your Route If the test center is not located at your school, you will need to become familiar with the area and plan your route. Think about the flow of traffic, the availability of parking, and the accessibility of public transportation.

Meals That Are Good For You Before the test, eat a meal that is both nutritious and balanced. Stay away from foods that are dense or high in sugar because they can cause your energy levels to plummet.

Techniques of Relaxation: In order to better deal with anxiety, try practicing some relaxation techniques, such as slow, deep breathing, mental imagery, or meditation.

Positive Mental Attitude It is important to keep a positive mental attitude and to constantly remind yourself of the things you have done to prepare. Have faith in your capabilities, and maintain your self-assurance.

The Day of the Exam

Get Up Early Give yourself plenty of time to get up, eat breakfast, and get ready for the day by getting up early. It's possible that being in a rush will increase your tension.

Comfortable Attire It is recommended that you go to the testing center wearing loose, comfortable clothing that can be layered in order to adapt to the temperature of the room.

Breakfast is the most important meal of the day, so make sure it's a nutritious one by including protein, complex carbohydrates, and fiber. This will assist in keeping your energy levels up over time.

Get an Early Start: Your goal should be to arrive at the testing facility with plenty of time to spare. It is preferable to arrive calm and collected at your destination if you do not have to rush there.

Identification: Please bring both your entry ticket and a current photo ID, in addition to any other items that may be requested by the testing center.

Perform a quick mental warm-up as part of the pre-exercise routine. To get you in the right frame of mind for the test, go over some practice questions.

Be Aware of Time: While taking the exam, make sure to keep track of the time allotted to each question and segment, and use it as effectively as possible.

Methods of Approaching Tests

Begin with Confidence It is important to begin the examination with confidence. Bring to mind your prior preparation and the questions you worked on in practice. If you get off to a good start on the test, it might do wonders for your confidence.

If you come across a question that is too difficult for you, you can skip it and come back to it later. You should put it off for now and come back to it later. Spending too much time thinking about a particular issue can waste valuable time.

Elimination Method: When trying to determine which of several possible answers is correct, use the method of elimination. The correct response can be more readily recognized as a result of this.

Take a few slow, deep breaths and bring your attention back to the task at hand whenever you feel the beginnings of worry creeping up on you. Breathing exercises that focus on control and mindfulness can both help alleviate anxiety.

Please Pay Close Attention to These Instructions: Take note of the instructions carefully before moving on to the next phase. There may be some variance in the timing and structure of the various components.

Mark Questions: If you are unsure about an answer, mark it as "uncertain" and move on to the next question. It is possible that returning to questions that have been marked at a later time with a new point of view will result in more accurate replies.

Utilize the Scratch Paper That Is Provided You can find scratch paper on the SSAT. Make use of time to work through the math problems, write down notes for the reading comprehension section, and prepare your thoughts for the writing sample.

Watch the clock carefully while you're working with the budget. Create a time budget for yourself so that you can finish each segment within the specified amount of time.

Maintain Your cool: If you run into a challenging question or area, maintain your cool. Your ability to find solutions to problems may suffer if you're anxious.

Review: If there is time left over at the end of a section, you should utilize it to review the questions and the answers you provided. Check for any mistakes or omissions in the information.

During the Pauses

The SSAT is broken up into multiple sections with brief intervals in between each one. Take this opportunity to relax and get ready for the next part of the lesson. During your breaks, you can perform the following:

Stretching: To relieve muscle tension, stand up and give your body a good stretching.

Drink plenty of water to stay hydrated, but steer away from drinks that contain an excessive amount of caffeine or sugar.

Snack: In order to keep your energy levels up, have a snack that is light and nutritious whenever you get the chance.

Resetting Your Mind: To reset your mind, and to remind yourself of your positive thinking and preparedness, read the following.

The Handling of Anxiety

The fear of performing poorly on a test is quite frequent, however there are ways to combat it:

Techniques involving breathing Deep, regulated breathing can help soothe the nerves. To relax, try taking several deep breaths.

Utilize positive self-talk, such as positive affirmations, to help raise your confidence. Remind yourself of your accomplishments and the skills you possess.

Visualization: Picture yourself succeeding in all you do. Imagine that you are able to confidently answer questions and that the test is very easy for you to finish.

Maintain your presence in the here and now to practice mindfulness. Don't get caught up in thinking about the questions that came before or the ones that come after.

Maintaining Progress: Maintaining progress through the test should be your primary focus as you work through each question in order.

After the Exam

After you have finished the SSAT, there are a few things that you should think about, including the following:

Maintain Your Calm: If you want to avoid needless tension, you should refrain from immediately discussing the test with your classmates.

Positive Reflection: Keep in mind that you should be proud of the fact that you did everything in your power. It is important to keep in mind that the SSAT is merely one component of the application process.

Take some time out for yourself to unwind and do something that brings you pleasure that is also peaceful.

Scores on Tests: Before making any decisions about retaking the SSAT, you should wait until your official test scores have been reported.

How to Make Sense of Your Results

It is imperative that you give careful consideration to how your SSAT scores should be interpreted once you have received them. Consider the following, among others:

Scores in Sections: Analyze the scores in each segment to determine where you excel and where you struggle in each domain.

Review your performance in light of your total score, which serves as a measure of how well you did overall.

Consider the percentile ranks to gain a better understanding of how your scores stack up in comparison to those of other people who took the test.

If you have used Score Choice, check to be that you have sent your top scores to schools depending on the policies that they have in place. This is especially important if you have utilized Score Choice.

Review the admissions procedures of the institutions to which you are applying in order to have an understanding of how the schools factor SSAT scores into the decision-making process for admitting students.

Taking the SSAT all over again

If you feel that your performance on the SSAT was not up to your expectations, you should think about taking it again. The following are some considerations to take into account:

Evaluate Your Potential for Improvement First, Evaluate Your Potential for Improvement. If you believe that more preparation can lead to better scores on the SSAT, then taking the exam more than once may be an option worth considering for you.

Deadlines for Schools: Check to be that the retake you plan to schedule coincides with the application deadlines of the schools to which you will be applying.

Limit the Number of Retakes You Take It is important to limit the number of retakes you take because certain schools look negatively upon students who take repeated exams. To improve your scores, you should concentrate on targeted preparation.

Score Choice Should you decide to retake the SSAT, you should use Score Choice to ensure that schools only receive your highest score.

Additional Resources is the topic of Chapter 11.

It is crucial to have access to a range of materials in order to strengthen your understanding of the test, reinforce your skills, and build your confidence while you are working through the process of preparing for the SSAT. This chapter gives an overview of useful extra resources that you can use to further enhance your preparation for the SSAT.

1. The Official Materials for the SSAT:

The institution responsible for the SSAT will offer you with official materials that are tailored to assist you in preparing for the examination. These resources include the following:

Official SSAT Practice Tests: These are the tests that come the closest to simulating the real SSAT. They feature questions and formats that are accurate for each portion of the exam.

The Official Guide to the SSAT is a detailed book that provides information about the SSAT, as well as practice questions and advice on how to perform well on the exam.

You can get official SSAT practice questions and exams online, giving you the opportunity to simulate test settings. The official online practice platform can be found here.

SSAT Student Guide: This guide offers an introduction of the SSAT, including instructions on how to register and a broad notion of what to anticipate on the day of the test.

It is strongly suggested that students use official SSAT resources because these materials are closely aligned with the actual test and provide an accurate test-taking experience.

2. Commercially Available Study Guides:

SSAT test preparation books are offered by a wide variety of businesses and publishers, and these books typically contain techniques, practice questions, and even full-length practice exams. Barron's, Kaplan, and The Princeton Review are just a few of the well-known publishers of test preparation materials. When selecting a commercial test preparation book, it is important to take into consideration a number of different aspects, including the publishing date, the specific level of the SSAT that the book covers (Elementary, Middle, or Upper), and user evaluations, in order to guarantee that the book is of sufficient quality and usefulness.

3. Websites Offering Online Practice:

There are a number of websites that offer resources for preparing for the SSAT online. Some of these websites provide practice questions and resources for free, while others demand a subscription or payment to access more thorough content in order to view it. Khan Academy, Testive, and Varsity Tutors are examples of websites that provide students with interactive courses, practice problems, and individualized study plans. When using online resources, you should be sure to choose platforms that correspond with both your preferred method of learning and your specific requirements.

4. Individualized Instruction and Practice Examinations:

The preparation for the SSAT can benefit from the individualized training and custom tactics that are offered by private tutoring and test prep programs. Your individual skills and weaknesses can be identified by tutors, and they can help you develop in those areas as you work together. Both in-person and online test preparation programs provide students with a curriculum that includes mock examinations and coaching from subject matter experts. If you require individualized attention or a regimented study plan, one of these choices may be a better fit for you than the others.

5. Vocabulary books and flashcards: both are available.

For the verbal portion of the SSAT, having a robust vocabulary is absolutely necessary for achievement. Building and enhancing your word knowledge can be accomplished with the use of flashcards and books of vocabulary. You can design your own vocabulary sets based on the vocabulary lists that are generally assessed on the SSAT, or you can use platforms like Quizlet that offer SSAT-specific vocabulary sets. Books on vocabulary, such as "Wordly Wise 3000" and "Barron's SAT Vocabulary," are another potential source of useful information.

6. Discussion Groups and Other Forms of Group Study:

It can be helpful to study alongside other students in the class. Participating in or organizing an SSAT study group gives you the opportunity to confer with others on tactics, exchange information, and conduct group exercises. You can seek guidance, share your experiences, and find solutions to your problems by visiting the specialized SSAT sections of online discussion forums such as College Confidential and Reddit.

7. Mobile Application:

There is a wide variety of software for mobile devices that can help students prepare for the SSAT. Apps for your smartphone or tablet such as "Magoosh: SAT & ACT Test Prep," "Varsity Tutors," and "Vocab Monster" provide you with practice questions, flashcards, and interactive courses to help you improve your vocabulary. These applications provide you more options for learning when you're on the road.

8. Workbooks for Practicing:

For each component of the SSAT—Verbal, Reading, Quantitative, and Writing—there is a corresponding practice booklet available for purchase. These workbooks will help you strengthen your abilities by providing you with additional practice questions, activities, and explanations. These resources are made available by well-known publishing houses such as Kaplan and McGraw-Hill.

9. Useful Free Resources Available Online:

There are some commercial resources available, but there are also numerous free online publications that can be useful for SSAT preparation. These are the following:

Sample Questions from Schools Several independent schools publish examples of SSAT questions on the websites of their respective organizations. These questions frequently mirror those that will be on the exam that you will have to take.

Educational YouTube Channels Channels on YouTube such as Khan Academy and CrashCourse offer video courses on a variety of subjects including mathematics, reading comprehension, and writing skills.

Websites Offering Free Lessons and activities Websites such as Purplemath and Grammarly offer free lessons and activities to help users improve their math and writing skills.

Online Practice exams There are a number of websites that provide online SSAT practice exams that can be utilized to imitate test conditions and evaluate your level of preparedness.

10. Preparation Courses for the SSAT:

Both in-person and online options are available for students interested in taking specialized SSAT prep classes. These classes are typically led by seasoned teachers who are conversant with the SSAT's structure as well as its subject matter. They may help you develop your skills by providing you with structured classes, practice assessments, and tailored feedback on your performance. The Princeton Review and Testmasters are only two of the most well-known companies that provide SSAT preparation courses.

11. Preparing for the SAT using College Board and Khan Academy:

There is a substantial amount of material and test-taking skill overlap between the SAT and the SSAT, despite the fact that the SSAT is a different test from the SAT. The College Board and Khan Academy have collaborated to provide students with free resources for SAT preparation. These resources include sample questions as well as full-length practice exams. Building your general math and reading skills that are applicable to the SSAT can be facilitated with the assistance of these tools.

12. Public Libraries in Your Area:

It's common practice for public libraries on a local level to have a selection of study materials available for checkout. In order to enhance your preparation for the SSAT, you can get books, workbooks, and other resources connected to the exam from the library.

13. School Counselors and Psychologists:

It's possible that the guidance counselors at your school have access to helpful resources, information, and advice pertaining to the SSAT. They may be able to offer advice regarding the examination as well as the application procedure for private schools.

14. The Scholastic Aptitude Test and Websites for Private Schools:

You can get extra information and resources by consulting the websites of the private institutions to which you are applying as well as the official website for the SSAT. Some institutions provide applicants with recommendations regarding what qualities they seek in applicants and how they evaluate SSAT scores.

15. Sample Essays and Prompts for Writing Practice:

Essay writing practice is absolutely necessary in order to prepare for the Writing Sample portion. You should look for essay ideas that are particular to the SSAT as well as general writing prompts that can assist you in developing your writing skills. Essay help and editing services are available online at websites such as PrepScholar and EssayEdge.

16. Textbooks for University Admissions:

works regarding the admissions process to colleges can provide useful insights into the qualities that colleges seek for in candidates, even though the SSAT is not the primary emphasis of these works. These books provide advice on how to write the essay for the application, how to do interviews well, and overall methods for admissions.

17. Information Regarding Accommodations for the SSAT Test:

If you have a disability that has been medically verified and require accommodations in order to take the SSAT, you will be able to request accommodations such as additional time, a reader, or a scribe. Those who are in need of accommodations may find it helpful to gain an understanding of the application procedure and the accommodations that are available.

Success Stories are covered in Chapter 12.

It is possible to achieve success in both the process of preparing for the SSAT and applying to private schools if one is dedicated, puts in a lot of effort, and uses the appropriate tactics. In this chapter, we will examine a collection of success stories from students who successfully navigated the SSAT process, received admission to their dream schools, and launched on a path to academic achievement. These students achieved their goals of achieving academic excellence while also gaining admission to their dream schools.

1. Emily's Struggles and Triumphs on the Road to a Prestigious Boarding School:

Emily, an ambitious eighth-grader, had her heart set on attending a famous boarding school that was well-known for its challenging academics and robust arts department. She was well aware of the significance that her performance on the SSAT would have on her application. The following are some of the most important steps along Emily's path to success:

Early Preparation: Emily started studying for the SSAT during the summer before she entered the eighth grade. Because she got a head start, she was able to gradually improve her talents over the course of time.

organized Study Plan Emily crafted an organized study plan for herself that included weekly tutoring sessions, practice tests, and official SSAT materials. Because of her strategy, she was able to thoroughly cover all of the test's different areas.

Practice in a Balanced Manner: In order to guarantee that no part of the SSAT was overlooked, she made sure to practice in a manner that was balanced throughout all of its areas, including Verbal, Reading, Quantitative, and Writing.

Ability to adapt: Emily often evaluated her progress and modified her study strategy so that it took into account both her strong and weak points. When it was required, she made adjustments in order to address tough regions.

Emily sought the mentorship of a previous SSAT tutor who had been successful in preparing children for elite boarding schools. Emily hoped to learn from this individual. The tutor offered individualized assistance and test-taking tactics to the student.

Emily kept a healthy mindset throughout her preparation by keeping a positive outlook on the situation and remaining motivated. She kept her attention on the objectives she had set for the long term and viewed obstacles as chances for personal development.

She always made sure to include time in her schedule to study for the SSAT, even at the times of the school year when she was the busiest. The effort and self-control paid off in the end.

Emily's preparation for the SSAT involved a lot of hard work and smart planning, which led to high marks and ultimately helped her gain admission to the boarding school of her choosing. She went on to achieve academic success and was quite active in the school's theater department after that.

2. Benjamin's Strides Towards Academic Accomplishment:

Benjamin, a kid in the seventh grade who had a strong interest in mathematics and wanted to pursue a career in the field, had his sights set on attending a highly exclusive private school that provided financial aid to exceptionally gifted pupils. The following procedures were included in his path to victory in the scholarship competition:

Benjamin began his evaluation by first submitting himself to a diagnostic SSAT practice test so that his academic strengths and shortcomings could be determined. Because of this evaluation, he was able to pinpoint the areas in which he needed to make improvements.

Targeted Preparation: Benjamin, based on the results of his assessment, concentrated his studying efforts on the quantitative portion of the exam. He sought out more math tasks and utilized resources that were particular to the SSAT.

Benjamin utilized online math platforms such as Khan Academy and IXL to further develop his math skills and to tackle more complicated mathematical ideas. These online tools are found on the internet.

Private Tutoring: Realizing the need of receiving individualized assistance, Benjamin hired a math tutor who was well-versed in the material covered on the SSAT. The tutor assisted the student by providing more practice questions as well as strategies for the examination.

Practice Exams: In order to get a feel for how the SSAT would be administered, Benjamin took a number of full-length practice exams. These exams helped him improve abilities in time management and built up his endurance for future tests.

In addition to his preparation for the SSAT, Benjamin participated in a series of simulated interviews in order to improve both his confidence and his presentation abilities in advance of his scholarship interviews.

Strong Application Essays Benjamin's application essays underlined his passion for mathematics and his desire to academic success. They also highlighted Benjamin's dedication to the field of mathematics. His essays highlighted the unique characteristics he possesses as well as the value he would provide to the institution if accepted.

Recommendations: Benjamin's professors and advisors offered excellent recommendations that emphasized his mathematical talents, work ethic, and potential for success in an academic environment that was tough.

The time and effort that Benjamin put into enhancing his mathematical abilities paid off. On the SSAT's quantitative portion, he performed exceptionally well, which resulted in numerous schools making scholarship offers to him. Benjamin was offered a scholarship to attend the school of his dreams, and he ultimately accepted it. There, he continued to perform exceptionally well in mathematics.

3. The Remarkable Changes Made by Sophia:

In the beginning of her preparation for the SSAT, Sophia, a student in middle school, ran into several difficulties. She battled with test anxiety, managing her time effectively, and the questions in the Verbal part. Nevertheless, the route she took to get where she is today is illustrative of the power that comes with tenacity and resilience. The subsequent events that led to Sophia's transformation are as follows:

Initial Difficulties: Sophia started her preparation for the SSAT with low scores on her practice tests. She frequently experienced feelings of being overpowered by the difficult terminology and analogies that were presented in the Verbal part.

The Practice of Mindfulness Sophia used practices from the practice of mindfulness to help manage her test anxiety. During the exam, she maintained her composure by engaging in deep breathing exercises and positive self-talk.

Assistance from a Tutor and Support: Since Sophia was aware of the challenges she faced, she decided to participate in an SSAT preparation course and seek assistance from a Verbal section tutor. The tutor suggested methods for tackling problems that were particularly difficult.

Development of Focused Vocabulary: Sophia spent more time concentrating on expanding her vocabulary. She learned new words and the meanings of those terms with the use of flashcards and vocabulary books.

Essays Written for Practice In order to enhance her performance in the Writing Sample area of the exam, Sophia periodically composed essays for practice and solicited feedback from her instructor. This helped her develop writing skills that were both clear and precise.

Thematic Reading: For the Thematic Reading section of the SSAT Reading test, Sophia concentrated her reading on books and articles that covered topics that are frequently covered in the reading passages. Because of this, her capacity to comprehend and evaluate difficult material increased.

Practice Reliably: Sophia set up a regular practice schedule for herself, which included taking timed practice portions as well as full-length practice tests.

Sophia gained the ability to stop comparing her own growth to that of others and instead concentrate on her own personal development. She also learnt the importance of setting realistic expectations for herself.

The results of Sophia's unrelenting dedication to her SSAT preparation were positive. Her performance on the practice tests continued to become better, and she felt less anxious as a result. As a result of her excellent performance on the Verbal portion of the test, Sophia was granted entrance to an elite private school. Her incredible comeback story proves that tenacity and hard work directed in the right direction may lead to accomplishment.

4. Noah's All-Encompassing Method for Achieving Excellence:

Noah, a very driven student who was in the sixth grade, set his sights on performing exceptionally well on the SSAT and gaining admission to a prestigious private school that had a robust scientific department. The following activities were a part of his all-encompassing strategy for preparing for the SSAT:

Early Start: Noah started his preparation for the SSAT early, during the summer before he entered the sixth grade. Because of this, he was able to steadily improve his abilities and his knowledge.

A Well-Rounded Approach: He allotted an equal amount of his study time to each component of the SSAT, devoting more of his focus to the Verbal, Reading, and Quantitative subtests while also ensuring that the Writing Sample received adequate consideration.

Time Management That Works: Noah devised a study regimen that helped him become better at managing the time he had available. While he was juggling his coursework and preparing for the SSAT, he set out certain time for each.

Official SSAT Materials: Noah prepared for the SSAT by taking official SSAT practice exams and reading The Official Guide to the SSAT. This allowed him to develop an understanding of the test's format as well as its subject matter.

Math Enrichment Noah saw that his love lay in the field of science, and in order to improve his mathematical abilities, he sought out further math enrichment classes and books.

Reading in Depth Practice: In order to increase his reading comprehension, he read a wide variety of books and articles covering a variety of scientific areas, in addition to reading works of literature.

Mock Interviews: Noah engaged in mock interviews with his teachers and mentors in order to prepare for the interview component of the admissions process. He was able to improve his poise and confidence as a result of these practice interviews.

Essays for Application Noah's application essays underlined his passion for science and his hopes to contribute to the academic community at the institution.

The amount of effort and thoroughness that Noah put into his SSAT preparation culminated in his receiving exceptional scores, which enabled him to successfully apply to the private school of his choosing. His continuing success in the science program at the school ultimately led to the accomplishment of his long-term objective of obtaining a position in the field of scientific research.

5. Isabel's Well-Rounded Strategy for Achieving Success:

Isabel, a talented and hard-working student, had her sights set on getting into a prestigious private school that placed equal importance on both academics and participation in extracurricular activities. Her story of achievement was molded by the well-rounded strategy she used to preparing for the SSAT:

Isabel developed a study regimen that allowed her to adequately prepare for the SSAT while also allowing her to maintain a healthy balance between her academic and extracurricular obligations. Because of this, she was able to keep up the appearance of a well-rounded person.

She relied on the official SSAT practice tests and The Official Guide to the SSAT to provide her with an accurate understanding of the exam material as well as a crystal clear comprehension of the test layout.

Participation in Extracurricular Activities Isabel maintained her level of involvement in the extracurricular activities offered at her school, exhibiting both her leadership abilities and her commitment to pursuing her interests.

Strong references were submitted by her instructors and mentors, highlighting her contributions to the school community as well as her academic success.

Enhancement of the Writing Sample Isabel's primary focus was on enhancing her writing sample by developing her writing skills via the practice of producing essays and soliciting comments from her instructors and tutors.

Meditation and other stress-reduction approaches, such as relaxation exercises, were among the practices she engaged in on a regular basis in order to better manage her exam anxiety.

good Attitude Isabel kept a good attitude throughout the application process and was aware that her application should represent the true interests and personality that she possesses.

Isabel's preparation for the SSAT and her application to the private school were both successful because she used a well-rounded approach. Because of the effort she put into both her studies and her extracurricular activities, she was considered a well-rounded applicant, which resulted in her being accepted to the school of her choice.

Test Modifications and Accommodations, Chapter 13

Students who have been medically diagnosed with a disability need to be provided with appropriate accommodations in order to take standardized exams on an equal footing with their classmates. One example of such a test is the Scholastic Aptitude Test (SSAT). This chapter will discuss the notion of test accommodations, the several sorts of accommodations that are offered for the SSAT, the application procedure, and the benefits that test accommodations offer to students.

Acquiring Knowledge about Accommodations for Tests

Individuals who have impairments are guaranteed an equal opportunity to demonstrate their knowledge and abilities through the use of test accommodations. These accommodations can take the form of changes or alterations made to standardized tests. The purpose of these accommodations is to remove or lessen the impact of a student's disability so that they are able to concentrate more on the material and abilities that are being evaluated by the test rather than on the difficulties they face as a result of their disability.

The purpose of providing students with disabilities with test accommodations is not to give them an unfair advantage; rather, they are to level the playing field for those kids. They are intended to align with the unique needs of a student, as described in the student's documentation of disability; nonetheless, they are not permitted to change the construct that is being tested by the test.

The various types of test accommodations that are available for the SSAT

The Secondary School Admission Test (SSAT) provides candidates who are qualified with a variety of testing accommodations. The following areas can be considered sub-categories of these accommodations:

1. Additional Time An additional allotment of time is one of the most typical accommodations that is granted for standardized examinations. Students who have disabilities are given an additional amount of time, often equal to fifty percent more time, to complete each component of the exam. If the typical time allotted for a part is 30 minutes, for instance, a student who has been granted more time would have 45 minutes to complete the section.

2. Students who have a medical condition or another impairment and require frequent breaks as a result of their condition may be eligible to receive additional break time. During the test, the students will have several breaks to refresh themselves and refocus their attention.

3. Exams Conducted in Small Groups Anxiety, sensory sensitivities, and other conditions might make it difficult for some students to perform well in exams that are administered in big groups. The testing is done in smaller groups, which creates an environment that is calmer and less overpowering.

4. Use of a Computer: It may be helpful for students who have specific limitations to type their comments on a computer rather than writing them by hand. This accommodation is especially relevant for the section on Writing Samples.

5. Screen Reading Software It is possible to equip students who have certain learning challenges or visual impairments with screen reading software that will read the test questions and passages out loud to them. Students who have difficulties reading or seeing will not have any trouble accessing the test thanks to this accommodation.

6. Materials Available in Braille or Large Print Students who have vision impairments have the option of receiving the exam materials in Braille or in a larger print size, depending on their personal preference and the requirements of the exam.

7. Help with the Marking Process Due to physical impairments, certain students may need assistance when it comes to marking their answers on the exam. This assistance can be provided by a specific individual without having an impact on the student's overall performance.

8. Provide Students Who Are Unable to utilize regular Test Booklets With Alternate Test Formats If a student is unable to utilize regular test booklets, they may be provided with alternate test formats such as electronic files, tactile visuals, or audio recordings.

Qualifications Required to Receive Exam Accommodations

Students with disabilities are required to present verification of their condition and complete certain qualifying requirements in order to get test accommodations for the SSAT. The following activities are normally required to complete the eligibility process:

1. Submission of Documentation of handicap In order to participate in the SSAT program, students are required to present documentation of their handicap. This paperwork should be provided by a trained practitioner, such as a physician, psychologist, or educational diagnostician, and it should clearly define the student's condition as well as the impact that the student's handicap has on their ability to take tests.

2. documents analyze and Student Eligibility Assessment The SSAT program will analyze the student's documents in order to determine whether or not the student is eligible for accommodations. They take into account the nature and degree of the handicap, the accommodations that were sought, and the potential influence that this could have on the construct that the test is measuring.

3. Determination and Approval: After the evaluation is complete, the SSAT program will reach a determination regarding whether or not the student is qualified to receive accommodations. In the event that the accommodations are allowed, a formal accommodation plan will detail the specific arrangements.

The Advantages of Providing Accommodations for Tests

Students who have impairments receive various important benefits in the form of test accommodations, which in turn helps these students perform to the best of their abilities on standardized exams such as the SSAT and others.

1. Equal Opportunity: Accommodations guarantee that students with disabilities have an equal opportunity to display their skills and knowledge

without being inhibited by the consequences of their disabilities. This is the first and most important goal of providing accommodations for students with disabilities.

2. Decreased Worry About Tests: Many students who have impairments have exam anxiety as a result of the difficulties they face as a result of their handicap. The use of accommodations can make students feel less anxious, which in turn allows them to concentrate more on the actual material being tested on.

3. Greater Accuracy Because of concessions such as additional time, students are able to take their time to fully comprehend the exam questions and provide answers that are more correct. This allows for a more accurate evaluation of their capabilities as a result.

4. enhanced Confidence: Students who are granted accommodations typically report feeling an enhanced level of confidence in their ability to perform on standardized tests. The enhanced performance may be a direct result of this increase in self-assurance.

5. Accessibility Students with a variety of disabilities, including as reading and vision impairments, are provided with accommodations so that they are able to take the exam. These accommodations can take the form of screen reading software or materials printed in a larger font size.

6. Fair Evaluation: The SSAT ensures that students with disabilities are judged fairly, on the basis of their genuine abilities, rather than on the consequences that their handicap has on them by offering accommodations, which allow them to take the test.

The Procedure for Submitting Applications for Exam Accommodations

There are multiple steps involved in the application procedure for test accommodations on the SSAT, and it is imperative that this process be started well in advance of the actual test date:

1. Acquire the Necessary Documentation The first step is to acquire the necessary documentation of your handicap. This paperwork ought to be as recent as possible, preferably within the past three years, and ought to have been drafted by an experienced expert. It needs to provide a detailed description of your handicap, the impact it has on taking tests, and the adjustments that are advised.

2. Get in touch with the program for the SSAT: Make contact with the SSAT program in order to get the request for an accommodation started. On the official website of the SSAT, you will normally be able to locate the contact information. The program will supply you with the essential instructions as well as the forms that are required for your request.

3. Fill out all of the necessary forms to request accommodations: Complete the necessary paperwork that has been sent to you by the SSAT program. These forms could include one for the parent or guardian, as well as one for the school. On these forms, it is absolutely necessary to supply information that is both correct and detailed.

4. Provide Documentation To the SSAT Program Please provide the SSAT program with any documentation of your impairment, any completed forms, and any other items that may be asked. Be careful to have this done in plenty

of time before the date you want to take the test so that there is enough time for processing.

5. Wait for a Decision: The SSAT program will consider your request for accommodations and study the material you have provided. They will communicate their decision to you, which may be an endorsement of the request or a rejection of it.

6. Arrange Your Test Date If your request for an accommodation is granted, you will need to coordinate with the SSAT program to arrange a test date that meets all of your requirements. Be sure that you are familiar with the specific adjustments that will be made for you on the day of the test.

7. Familiarize Yourself with Your Accommodations It is really important to become acquainted with the accommodations that you will be provided with. You should get some experience with the technologies or assistive equipment you plan to use in a testing environment before the big day so that everything goes as smoothly as possible.

8. Communicate with institutions If you want to transmit your SSAT scores to private institutions, you should inform those schools about the accommodations you will be receiving before you send the scores. This makes certain that the schools are aware of the adjustments and that they are able to give additional help in the event that it is required.

Concerns and Things to Take Into Account

Students with disabilities have access to a vital resource in the form of test accommodations; nonetheless, there are some problems and considerations that should be kept in mind:

1. Requirements for paperwork The paperwork of the handicap needs to be up to date and it needs to meet a certain set of standards. The process of collecting and submitting the necessary documentation can be one that is both time-consuming and laborious.

2. Time Required for Processing: The procedure for submitting an application for accommodations may take many weeks or even months. It is essential to get the procedure started as soon as possible in order to guarantee that the necessary accommodations will be in place for the test day that you desire.

3. Stigma and Misconceptions: There is a possibility that some families and students will be concerned about the potential stigma that is connected with asking adjustments. It is necessary to keep in mind that accommodations are not an admission of inability but rather exist to provide equal chances. It is important to keep this in mind.

4. Specific Requirements Accommodations are very customized and ought to be tailored to meet the particular requirements of the learner. The appropriate accommodations for one student can seem very different from those ideal for another.

5. Communication with Schools You need to make sure that you speak with the schools that you are applying to about the adjustments that you require. During the admissions process, this may enable institutions to provide additional support to applicants.

Techniques for Managing Your Time and Studying Effectively is the Topic of Chapter 14.

The key to successful preparation for the SSAT is in the utilization of efficient time management and study methods. In this chapter, we will discuss many methods that can assist students in making the most of their time spent studying and developing the abilities essential to perform well on the SSAT.

The Importance of Effective Time Management and Different Methods of Studying

The process of preparing for the SSAT is a substantial task that calls for attentive planning, unwavering focus, and methodical study. Techniques of effective time management and study are necessary for a number of reasons, including the following:

Learning Is Optimized When Students Use Effective Study approaches Effective study approaches assist students successfully absorb and retain information, ensuring that their study time is fruitful.

Consistency: Effective time management enables students to have a constant study schedule, which is essential for remembering previously learned information and increasing one's skills over the course of one's academic career.

Reducing tension: Students who have good time management are better able to approach tests with confidence and experience less of the tension that is associated with cramming at the last minute.

Adaptability: Students are better able to concentrate on improving areas in which they struggle if they have the ability to modify their study strategies to address specific gaps in knowledge.

Finding a Happy Medium Many students taking the SSAT have intense academic work as well as commitments to extracurricular activities. They are able to create a balance between their academics and their other commitments with the assistance of time management tools.

Techniques for Managing One's Time

Setting specific goals, developing a study schedule, and putting into action various tactics to make the most of available study time are all essential components of efficient time management. Consider implementing some of the following time management strategies:

Setting Objectives:

Establish Well-Defined Goals: Outline what you need to do and define the goals you have for the SSAT, such as your target scores for each part.

In order to make it less difficult to monitor your advancement toward your objectives, you need first break your goals down into more achievable subgoals.

Create a Timeline: Construct a study timeline that includes exact dates for accomplishing each of these objectives.

Developing a Timetable for Your Studies:

Plan for Weekly Studying You should create a weekly calendar that allots certain blocks of time for SSAT preparation and stick to it. Think about how available you are as well as how much energy you have at different times of the day.

Maintaining a productive routine requires that you be as consistent with your plans as you possibly can if you want to see results.

Include rests: To prevent mental burnout and improve attention, it is important to include brief rests in between periods of study.

Establishing Priorities and Organizing:

Identify the aspects of your knowledge that need the most improvement and devote a greater portion of your study time to improving those areas.

Make use of To-Do Lists: Whether you choose to create them on a daily or weekly basis, To-Do Lists are an effective tool for organizing and prioritizing tasks.

area for Studying: Ensure that your study area is well-organized and devoid of any potential sources of distraction.

Blocking out time:

Your study time should be segmented into concentrated blocks that are dedicated to specific themes or sections of the SSAT. Divide the total amount of time you have available to study into these blocks.

Maintain Your Focus: During each of the allotted time blocks, your complete attention should be focused on the work at hand. Stay away from multitasking if you want to maintain your level of productivity.

Reconsider and Modify:

Regular Evaluations You should evaluate your progress on a regular basis and make any necessary adjustments to your study routine and methods.

Adapt to Obstacles: If you run into trouble understanding certain concepts or sections of the material, set aside more time to study so that you can overcome those obstacles.

Ensure That Your Expectations Are Realistic:

Be practical: recognize your own rate of learning and establish objectives that are within your reach. Expectations that cannot be met may result in feelings of dissatisfaction and exhaustion.

Methods of Learning That Are Useful

The most efficient methods of studying improve both comprehension and recall. The following are some methods that will help you improve your approach to studying:

Learning Through Activity:

Engage with the Material In order to actively engage with the content, you should ask questions, take notes, and try to summarize the information using your own words.

Participate in Conversations and Debates: Participating in conversations or debates about the content helps to further one's grasp of it.

Exercise Yourself with Some Sample Questions:

Practice Tests By simulating the conditions of the real test and testing your ability to manage your time effectively, you can benefit from taking full-length practice tests.

Examine Your Errors You should examine your errors from the practice tests in order to comprehend why you got the questions wrong.

Mnemonic devices and flashcards:

Building Your Vocabulary: If you want to learn and retain vocabulary words, you can use flashcards. The use of mnemonics can assist in developing remember associations for difficult words.

Putting it all together:

Imagine in your mind other thoughts, graphs, or maps that are associated with the material. Memory is strengthened by the use of visualization.

The process of:

The content should be divided such that large amounts of information are broken down into smaller, more manageable pieces. Because of this, it is now easy to absorb and keep.

Instructing Other People:

Teach a Friend: Providing an explanation of a subject to a close friend or member of your family can help you to better comprehend that concept yourself.

Participatory Reading:

Texts can be annotated by highlighting and underlining essential points, jotting down summaries or questions in the margins, and highlighting and underlining relevant material as it is read.

Learning Through Multiple Senses:

Employ a Number of Senses: When you're trying to learn something new, you should try activities that engage a number of your senses, such as sketching diagrams, viewing instructional videos, or listening to podcasts.

Methods of Studying Tailored to the Exam

Methods of preparation that are specific to each portion of the SSAT are required:

Verbal Constituents:

Develop Your Vocabulary: Make it a priority to broaden your vocabulary by picking up new terms, gaining a knowledge of what those words imply, and engaging in analogy practice.

Reading Comprehension: To improve your reading comprehension, try summarizing each paragraph as you read it. This will help you become more comfortable reading and understanding longer sections.

Reading Part: [Chapter]

During active reading, you can increase your comprehension by underlining or highlighting important ideas in the texts you are reading.

Skills in Inferencing: Train yourself to be able to draw conclusions from a text by forecasting the results, determining the relationship between causes and effects, and grasping the author's point of view.

The quantitative section consists of:

Fundamentals of Mathematics Conducting a review of fundamental mathematical concepts and formulas is an excellent way to fortify your foundation.

Problem-Solving: Pay attention to different problem-solving tactics and practice a wide variety of mathematical conundrums.

A Sample of Writing:

Structure of an Essay: Become familiar with and practice the structure of a well-organized essay, which includes the introduction, body paragraphs, and conclusion.

Clarity and Conciseness: When writing, make it a point to practice being clear and succinct, avoiding unnecessarily complicated sentences.

Exam Preparation Strategies Regarding Time Management

The taking of practice exams is an essential component of getting ready for the SSAT. Your ability to imitate test settings and develop your test-taking skills depends on your ability to effectively manage time during practice tests. The following is a list of suggestions for effective time management during practice tests:

Create a Simulation of the Actual Testing Conditions:

You should take your practice exams in an area that is free of noise and other distractions.

Start a timer and adjust it so that it corresponds to the allotted amount of time for each part of the official test.

Observe the Time Limits Set by the Officials:

Be sure to observe the prescribed time limitations for each part of the test, including any breaks that may be included.

You should fight the urge to go on to the next segment even if you finish one before the allotted time even if you finish one early. Make use of the time that is left to look over your work.

Keep an Eye on Your Advancement:

Keep a record of the times you started and stopped each segment. This can help you evaluate how well you are able to manage your time.

If there is a segment in which you routinely come up short on time, you should work on developing techniques to increase your speed.

Dealing with Anxiety:

Make use of tactics for relaxation, such as taking deep breaths, in order to control exam anxiety and keep your attention.

Determine your priorities:

Determine how much time to spend on each question based on the number of points it's worth. For the Quantitative section of the exam, for instance, you should give more weight to the problems that carry a greater point value.

Move On and Continue:

If you come into a question that is difficult, you shouldn't spend an excessive amount of time on it. You can skip it and come back to it later if you have time after you've answered the other questions.

Maintain Your Uniformity:

Your ability to effectively manage time can be improved by regularly exercising under timed situations.

Preparing for the SSAT While Juggling Other Responsibilities

Many students taking the SSAT lead hectic lifestyles that are filled with coursework, extracurricular activities, and obligations to their families. It is essential to strike a balance between preparing for the SSAT and one's other duties in order to avoid being overwhelmed and to keep up a healthy way of life:

Set your priorities, and then plan:

Make a list of your top priorities, which should include schooling, preparing for the SSAT, and any other commitments you have.

Develop a plan for the week that specifies how much time will be spent on each priority.

Blocking out time:

Make use of time-blocking in order to assign particular periods of time to preparing for the SSAT, doing assignments, and other things.

Ensure that your daily schedule is well-balanced by include both breaks and time for leisure.

Try to Find Help:

Talk to your parents, guardians, or teachers about the SSAT goals you have set for yourself and the support you need to better manage your time.

When necessary, look for help with your coursework or the commitments you've made outside of class.

Maintain your order:

Make use of planners, digital calendars, or to-do lists in order to keep track of study sessions, assignments, and deadlines related to the SSAT.

Keep your equilibrium:

Make taking care of yourself a top priority. This includes getting enough rest, eating well, and staying active.

Reduce the amount of stress in your life by practicing relaxation techniques such as meditation or mindfulness.

Dealing with Test Anxiety, which is Chapter 15 of the Book

When it comes to preparing for standardized examinations like the SSAT, a major obstacle that many students must overcome is test anxiety. In this chapter, we will discuss the notion of test anxiety, as well as its effects on performance on tests, as well as techniques to effectively manage and overcome test anxiety.

Comprehending the Fear of the Exam

The sensations of unease, fear, and stress that students experience prior to, during, or after taking a test are collectively referred to as test anxiety. When it gets overpowering, this anxiety can have a substantial impact on a student's ability to demonstrate their genuine talents on the SSAT. Anxiety can be a natural response to the pressure of performing well.

Anxiety over taking a test can appear in a number of different ways, including behavioral symptoms (such as fidgeting and avoidance behaviors), cognitive symptoms (such as negative self-talk and racing thoughts), and physical symptoms (such as a quick heartbeat, nausea, and perspiration). It could be induced by a variety of circumstances, such as the dread of failing the test, having high expectations for oneself, or not knowing what would be on the test.

The Influence that Test Anxiety Has on One's Performance on the SSAT

Anxiety before exams can have a number of negative effects on performance on the SSAT, including the following:

Reduced Concentration Anxiety might make it difficult to focus on the questions and passages that are being asked on the test, which can lead to misunderstandings and mistakes.

Memory Impairment High levels of anxiety can make it difficult to recollect memories, which can make it difficult to remember things like facts, formulae, or vocabulary.

Processing Speed Can Be Slowed Down Anxiety has been shown to slow down cognitive processing, which can lead to difficulties with managing time while taking an exam.

Reduced Self-Confidence: Anxiety can lead to self-doubt, which increases the likelihood that students will change their accurate responses or second-guess their own answers.

Physical Symptoms The presence of anxiety can manifest itself in a variety of painful and distracting physical symptoms, such as a racing heart or feelings of nausea.

Negative Self-Talk Students who are anxious about their performance on a test are more likely to engage in negative self-talk, which increases the likelihood that they will perform poorly.

Techniques for Overcoming the Fear of the Exam

One of the most important aspects of SSAT preparation is learning how to control test anxiety. The following are some ways that can assist students in lowering their test-related anxiety and improving their overall performance:

Complete your preparations:

The most effective method for reducing test anxiety is to adequately prepare for the test. When pupils have the impression that they have adequately prepared, they have more faith in their own capabilities.

Study the following, as it will appear on the Exam:

Utilize the official SSAT practice tests and materials so that you can grow accustomed to the test's structure, the different sorts of questions, and the time constraints. The more you understand about the test, the more confident you'll feel going into it.

Make a Study Plan That Includes:

Anxiety can be reduced by using an organized study plan that goes over all of the test portions and gradually builds up skills. You will be well prepared for the exam if you have a detailed plan.

Exercises to Simulate the Test Environment:

Participate in mock examinations under conditions that more closely resemble the real test, such as strict time limits and an unbroken lack of background noise. You will become more comfortable with the testing process as a result of doing this.

Talking to Oneself Favorably:

Positive affirmations should be used in place of negative self-talk. Confronting negative attitudes with positive thoughts about one's capabilities can be quite freeing.

Practices That Help You Relax:

To better control anxiety and keep one's attention, it can be helpful to practice relaxation techniques such as slow, deep breathing, meditation, or progressive muscle relaxation.

Management of One's Time:

For each part of the exam, you should work on developing good time management abilities. Effective time management alleviates the stress that comes with feeling rushed all the time.

Imagine yourself succeeding:

Imagine yourself doing well on the test by employing several types of visualization strategies. Creating mental images that are upbeat and uplifting might help build confidence.

Be Sure to Put Your Health and Sleep First:

In the days coming up to the exam, making sure you receive enough rest should be your first priority. A mind that has been properly rested is one that is better able to deal with stress.

Maintain Your Health:

In order to enhance your general well-being, you should stick to a balanced diet and an exercise program. The state of one's mental health can be affected by one's physical health.

Reduce Your Intake of Caffeine and Sugar:

Caffeine and sugar are two things that should be avoided before a test because they can both contribute to heightened anxiety and jitters.

Maintain an optimistic and practical outlook:

Maintain a constructive attitude on your capabilities, but do not lose sight of the importance of setting reasonable goals. Recognize that you, like everyone else, are not flawless and that it is acceptable to make errors.

Try to Find Help:

Discuss your anxiety with close loved ones, close friends, or a professional counselor. Talking about your worries can provide you with some much-needed emotional support.

Help from Qualified Individuals:

Consider getting professional help from a therapist or counselor who specializes in anxiety disorders if your test anxiety is overwhelming and continues even after you've finished the exam.

Practices of Mindfulness and Mind-Body Integration:

Participate in activities such as yoga, tai chi, or meditation to develop your awareness and lower your anxiety levels.

Techniques for Overcoming Anxiety on the Day of the Test

On the day of the test, certain tactics can help you manage your nervousness and perform at your absolute best:

go There Early: Make it a priority to go to the testing location in plenty of time to spare. The stress caused by being late to a test can be increased.

Maintain Your Calm Before entering the testing facility, take a few moments to perform some deep breathing exercises or other relaxation techniques.

Pay Attention to the Here and Now: Instead of worrying about questions that you haven't encountered yet, give your full attention to the one that is currently in front of you.

Affirmations Positives: Remind yourself of the preparation you've put in, and confirm your own capabilities. Anxiety can be alleviated by maintaining a positive attitude.

Comfort in the body Be sure to dress in comfortable clothes and carry layers with you in case the temperature in the testing room is not to your liking. Anxiety can be alleviated by comfort.

Adhere to Your pattern: If you want to feel more at ease and familiar with your surroundings, try following the same pattern every morning.

Drink plenty of water and have a snack that's not too heavy before the exam so that you can keep your mind clear and your energy up.

Time Management: Determine how much time you will need depending on the total number of questions and the points that each question is worth. You shouldn't let yourself become fixated on a particular question; instead, move on and come back if necessary.

Maintain a positive attitude, and if you are confronted with a difficult question, try not to dwell on it. Maintain an optimistic attitude, and move on to the next challenge.

Techniques for Breathing: If you start to feel worried while taking the test, pause for a moment and take a few long, deep breaths to regain your composure.

Managing Your Anxiety on the Day of the Exam

On the day of the test, it is typical to experience at least some nervousness, even with the best preparation and techniques. Additional strategies to combat the anxiety associated with test day are as follows:

Recognize That It Is Normal to Feel Nervous Before a Significant Test: Recognize that it is normal to feel nervous before a significant test. Recognize that the way you're feeling is a perfectly normal reaction to the stressful circumstance you're in.

Maintain your presence in the here and now and focus your attention on the problem at hand. Reducing anxiety can be helped by keeping one's attention on the activity at hand.

Always Keep Things in Perspective: The SSAT is Just One element of Your Academic Journey Keep in mind that the SSAT is just one element of your academic journey. It is not indicative of your value or of your potential for future achievement.

Believe in Your Preparation You should have faith in the preparations you've made for the test and the hard work you've put into it. Your time spent practicing and putting in effort will be rewarded.

Make the Most of Your Tactics: Make use of the strategies for relaxation and encouraging good self-talk that you have been working on during your preparation.

Maintain a Resilient perspective: When confronted with challenging questions, it is important to keep a resilient perspective. Take a proactive approach to tackling the issues they raise.

If your nervousness becomes too much to handle and begins to influence your performance on the test, you should seriously consider having a conversation about it with a test proctor or someone from the testing center.

Discussion Following the Test

Regardless of how anxious you were before taking the SSAT, you should be sure to give some thought to how well you performed on the exam once you've finished. The act of reflecting can yield useful insights that can be applied to future test-taking experiences:

Evaluate How Well You Have Done: Think about the aspects of your test-taking tactics that worked well and those that could use some work.

Examine any errors that were committed during the test and try to figure out why you got particular questions wrong. This is the best way to learn from your mistakes.

Adjust Your Test Preparation and Anxiety Management techniques for Future Tests: In order to adapt your test preparation and anxiety management techniques for future tests, you should use the experience you gained from this one.

Maintain a happy Attitude: Regardless of how well you performed, you should always keep a happy attitude. Your future achievements are not going to be determined by a single test, so use each examination as a learning opportunity.

Advanced Math Concepts are Covered in Chapter 16

The purpose of the Quantitative component of the SSAT is to evaluate a student's mathematical skills. This section of the exam consists of questions that cover a wide variety of subject areas. In this chapter, we will discuss advanced mathematical ideas and tactics that students can use to better prepare for and perform better on the SSAT's most difficult quantitative problems.

Concepts of a More Advanced Nature on the SSAT Math Exam

The Student Scholastic Aptitude Test (SSAT) has a portion called Quantitative that evaluates a student's ability to do mathematical tasks such as arithmetic, algebra, geometry, and data analysis. There are some questions on the SSAT that expect you to have a better comprehension of more advanced mathematical topics, even if the majority of the questions on the exam are at a middle school level. These problems are intended to present a difficult challenge to students who already possess a high level of mathematical proficiency.

The following are some of the more sophisticated mathematical ideas that could be tested on the SSAT:

Manipulation of Algebraic Expressions Solving equations with variables on both sides, factoring, and working with algebraic expressions are examples of the kind of questions that may be asked in advanced algebra.

Equations Quadratic The students could run into problems that need them to solve quadratic equations by employing strategies such as factoring, the quadratic formula, or completing the square.

Exponents and Radicals: There is a possibility that students will be asked questions that use exponents, roots, and logarithms. These questions will test the students' comprehension of these concepts as well as their ability to simplify equations.

Coordinate Geometry: Students who are working on more advanced problems in coordinate geometry may be required to deal with equations of lines, determine the distances between points, and recognize geometric shapes in the coordinate plane.

Ratios and Proportions at an Advanced Level Some of the questions will include complex ratio and proportion issues, the solutions to which will frequently need numerous stages.

Students may be required to work with complex fractions, decimals, and percentages, including repeated and terminating decimals. Additionally, students may be required to work with percentages.

Concepts Related to Advanced Geometry Concepts related to advanced geometry may include congruence, similarity, the Pythagorean theorem, and geometric transformations.

Questions pertaining to data analysis may entail reading and working with graphs, charts, and tables that are more complicated, as well as understanding concepts such as probability and statistics.

Methods for Confronting More Advanced Mathematical Concepts

To assure one's success on the SSAT when dealing with more difficult mathematical ideas, it is necessary to approach these problems with a well-defined plan in order to answer them. Students will benefit from the following tactics while tackling more advanced mathematical concepts:

Comprehend the Foundational Concepts It is important to ensure that you have a strong foundation in the fundamental mathematical concepts, as these notions serve as the building blocks for more complex courses.

Spend some time going over more difficult mathematical ideas and then put your knowledge to the test by working through some relevant practice problems. Make use of the practice materials provided by the SSAT in order to get accustomed to the format of the advanced questions.

Work Through Examples: To show how more complicated issues are addressed step by step, use the worked examples provided in textbooks or in online resources.

Simplify Equations In order to solve algebraic equations, you must first simplify them by grouping terms that are similar and isolating the variables. Equations become easier to work with as a result of this.

Utilize Algebraic Techniques When doing algebraic manipulations, it is necessary to make use of algebraic techniques such as factoring, completing the square, and utilizing the quadratic formula where appropriate.

Be Familiar with Geometric Properties In order to answer questions on geometry, you should be familiar with the characteristics of geometric shapes as well as the connections between lines, angles, and other geometric components.

Create Diagrams: To better visualize the issue, create diagrams or sketches whenever it is suitable to do so. This may assist you in better comprehending concepts relating to geometry or space.

Estimation: When working with complicated equations or numbers, estimation can help you swiftly remove solution alternatives that are erroneous and narrow down your options.

Develop your ability to perform calculations in your head by engaging in mental arithmetic practice. This is especially helpful when working with fractions, decimals, and percentages.

Verify That Your Work: Always perform a second check of your work, but this is especially important for more complex situations that may require numerous phases. Make sure that the response you provided to the question is accurate.

Try a Number of alternative Methods: If you're having trouble finding a solution to a problem, you should try a number of alternative methods or approaches to see if any of them can help.

Maintaining composure is an essential part of overcoming exam anxiety when facing difficult arithmetic problems. Even when confronted with difficult challenges, remember to take a few slow, deep breaths and keep a level head.

Examples of Problems in Advanced Mathematics

Let's have a look at some sample problems in advanced mathematics that might be asked on the SSAT:

The first question is on algebra.

Find the solution for

$3x-5=2(x+4)-7$

The second question is in geometry.

The length of one leg of a right triangle is five units, whereas the length of the hypotenuse is thirteen units. What is the total length of both legs together?

Analysis of the Data (Question 3)

75% of people who responded to a survey claimed that they enjoy chocolate, while 60% said that they prefer vanilla. What is the highest possible percentage of responders that could have a preference for chocolate and vanilla?

Ratios and proportions are the topics of the fourth question.

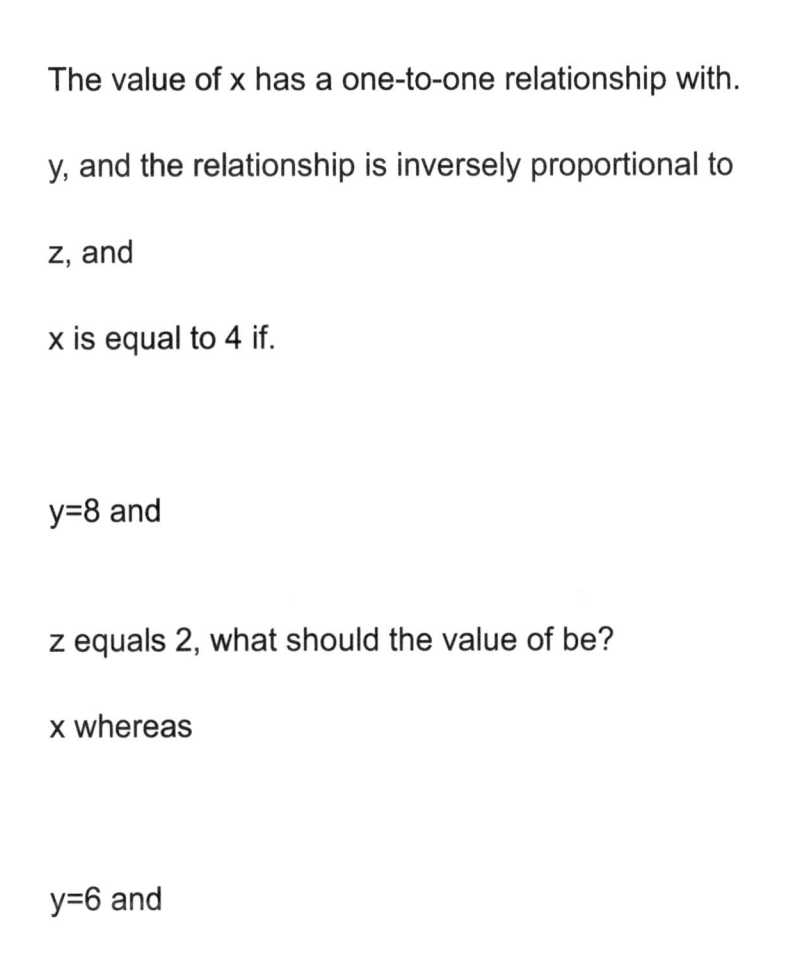

The value of x has a one-to-one relationship with.

y, and the relationship is inversely proportional to

z, and

x is equal to 4 if.

y=8 and

z equals 2, what should the value of be?

x whereas

y=6 and

The fifth question concerns radicals and exponents.

Make it easier:

Coordinate geometry is the topic of the sixth question.

The points' respective coordinates

A and

B in the plane of the coordinates are

(3,4) and

(respectively minus one and two). How far apart are the two sites in question?

A and

These sample problems provide students with an illustration of the kinds of advanced mathematical ideas that could appear on the SSAT. In order to properly solve these problems, you will need enough of practice as well as a solid understanding of the essential mathematical ideas.

Extra Mathematical Resources for the More Advanced Concepts

Consider making use of additional resources, such as the following examples, to further improve your comprehension of more sophisticated mathematical concepts:

Textbooks Covering Advanced Math Concepts You should look for math textbooks or study aids that cover advanced math concepts. Detailed explanations and practice problems are frequently available from the aforementioned venues.

Mathematical Resources Available Online Investigate the various online math platforms and websites that include walkthroughs, interactive lessons, and practice problems on more complex mathematical ideas.

Competitions in Mathematics If you want to be exposed to increasingly difficult mathematical problems, you should think about competing in mathematics competitions or joining mathematics clubs.

Personal Tutoring: If you are having a particularly difficult time grasping advanced mathematical topics, working with a personal math tutor can offer you with the individualized direction and help you need.

Participate in Math Communities and Discussion Boards By participating in math communities and discussion boards, you will have the opportunity to talk about more advanced mathematical concepts, ask questions, and learn from more experienced mathematicians.

Expanding Your Vocabulary is the Topic of Chapter 17

A robust vocabulary is an invaluable advantage in many facets of life, including achieving one's academic goals and performing well on standardized examinations such as the SSAT. In this chapter, we will discuss the significance of vocabulary on the SSAT, several tactics for expanding one's vocabulary, and effective ways to incorporate newly learned terms into one's regular speech.

The Role of Vocabulary in the Scholastic Aptitude Test

The vocabulary of a student is evaluated using several different portions of the SSAT, including the Verbal section, the Reading section, and the Analytical Writing section. Because of the following factors, having a robust vocabulary is absolutely necessary for doing well on the SSAT:

Reading Comprehension: Having a large vocabulary improves your capacity to comprehend and make sense of difficult literature. If you have a robust vocabulary, you will be able to determine the meanings of unknown words that appear in SSAT reading passages by analyzing the context in which they are used.

Verbal Section: The SSAT's Verbal section includes questions on synonyms and analogies, which need you to have a wide vocabulary in order to recognize and identify word links. This section of the exam is known as the "Verbal Section."

Essay Writing: In the Writing Sample part, having a strong vocabulary enables you to express ideas effectively, utilize precise language, and communicate clearly. In addition, it enables you to communicate more precisely.

When it comes to scoring, having a robust vocabulary will help you achieve a higher score on the SSAT. Your knowledge of word meanings is essential to providing accurate responses to questions in the Verbal and Reading domains.

Academic Performance: In addition to scoring well on the SSAT, having a large vocabulary is essential for being successful in school. It strengthens reading comprehension, writing skills, and the ability to communicate well with both instructors and classmates.

Methods that Can Help You Expand Your Vocabulary

The process of increasing one's vocabulary is one that is slow and continual, and it requires one to actively engage with words and the meanings of those words. The following are some proven methods that will help you expand your vocabulary:

Read extensively and consistently:

You will become familiar with a wide range of vocabulary and usages if you read things like books, newspapers, magazines, and articles found online. Pick books from a variety of categories and on a wide range of subjects to expand your vocabulary.

Learning Within Its Context:

Pay close attention to the ways in which sentences and paragraphs put words to use. The meanings of unknown words can often be deduced from the context in which they are used.

Maintain a Journal for Your Vocabulary:

Create and keep updated a vocabulary journal or notebook in which you can record new terms, their explanations, and examples of their use. Maintaining a consistent schedule of reading and editing the journal.

Make use of flashcards to:

Make some flashcards with a word and its definition printed on opposite sides. Conduct word meaning drills on a regular basis to improve your vocabulary.

Memory aids: mnemonic devices

When trying to remember the meanings of words, it can be helpful to employ memory aids such as acronyms, rhymes, or visual associations.

A Few Thematic Lists:

Create word lists based on topics, such as words associated with science, history, or literature, then organize these lists. This helps you categorize words and remember them based on the topics they share.

Resources Available Online for Vocabulary:

Explore many resources and tools that can help you develop your vocabulary online, such as websites, apps, and vocabulary games.

Put Words in Their Proper Context:

Make an effort to use new words in your writing as well as in conversation. Words are best understood and used when they are practiced in their natural environments.

The Word-a-Day Challenge consists of:

Put yourself to the test and try to pick up a new word every day. Find words that are either unusual or intriguing to you, make an effort to learn their definitions, and then utilize those words in your day-to-day talks.

Take Part in Quizzes and Other Competitions Regarding Vocabulary:

Put your knowledge to the test by participating in vocabulary quizzes and contests, either online or in your local community. This will force you to think outside of your comfort zone.

Read It Out Loud:

Reading out loud helps you better retain information by exposing you to the pronunciation of words and the context in which they are used in sentences.

The origin of the word:

Investigate the history of words, often known as their etymologies. The meanings of things can be better understood by first learning about their origins and histories.

Multiple and Varied Sources:

Read works that hail from a variety of cultural traditions and historical eras. You can expand both your vocabulary and your understanding of its intricacies by reading a wide variety of texts.

Talk About It and Argue About It:

Take part in debates and conversations with your contemporaries or members of your family. Words you might not normally use might come up in the course of a conversation.

Word Searches and Other Puzzles Involving Words:

For the purpose of expanding your vocabulary, try your hand at word puzzles like crosswords and games like Scrabble and Boggle.

Methods That Are Useful For The Acquisition Of Vocabulary

Think about the following strategies if you want to get the most out of your efforts to increase your vocabulary:

Review on a Regular Basis:

Reviewing your vocabulary diary or flashcards on a regular basis will help you better understand the meanings of individual words.

Submission of an Application in Writing:

Make use of the newly acquired vocabulary in the writing assignments you have. Because of this practice, you will be able to assimilate new terms into your working vocabulary.

Practical Application:

Include new vocabulary in the email exchanges, phone calls, and in-person chats that you have on a regular basis. Putting what you've learned into practice in realistic settings will help you remember it better and make better use of it.

A Sentence Containing the Word:

When you are trying to learn a new term, try working it into one of your own sentences. This clarifies the meaning of the word when placed in its appropriate context.

Antonyms and synonyms are as follows:

Comprehend the target term in addition to its antonyms and synonyms, which are words having meanings that are related to but not the same as the target word. This places things in a more comprehensive perspective for comprehension.

The Origins of Language:

Investigate the meanings of words by looking at their origins, prefixes, and suffixes. It is easier to comprehend a word's meaning if you are familiar with its constituent parts.

Expansion of Some Words Used as an Example

Here are some instances of expanding one's vocabulary by utilizing just a few words:

Word 1: Effortless eagerness

Definition: the state of being alert and cheerfully ready.

Example Sentence: She jumped at the chance to test her abilities and enthusiastically embraced the challenge.

Word 2: astutely perceptive

Definition: The quality of having a profound comprehension or perception.

Example Sentence: The astute detective was able to figure out what had happened quite quickly.

Word 3: in high spirits

Exuding boundless enthusiasm, excitement, or energy is the definition of bubbling over.

The jubilant celebration that the squad had after learning they had won the tournament was an example of how happy they were.

Quixotic is the fourth word.

The state of being excessively idealistic; the quality of being unrealistic and unpractical.

Example Sentence: While his idealistic intentions for world peace were certainly admirable, there were many obstacles that stood in the way of their actualization.

Ephemeral is the fifth word.

Definition: existing for just a relatively brief period of time; ephemeral.

Example Sentence: The fleeting beauty of the cherry blossoms serves as a constant reminder of how quickly life may change.

Word 6: To shroud in mystery

To intentionally muddle the meaning of something such that it cannot be understood.

Example Sentence The politician's attempt to obscure the true nature of the situation only served to increase popular mistrust.

Including Recently Acquired Words Into Everyday Conversations

Consider incorporating the following linguistic habits into your routine in order to integrate your newly acquired vocabulary into your regular speech:

Use it or lose it: Make an effort to incorporate new vocabulary into your daily writing and speech. Include them in the written work that you do as well as the conversations that you have daily.

Be Aware of Context It is important to be aware of the context in which the words you use are being used. This guarantees that you use them in the correct manner and to their full potential.

Utilizing new vocabulary on a regular basis will help strengthen both your understanding and your memory. Words can more easily get ingrained in your vocabulary through the use of repetition.

Experimenting with New Words in a Variety of Contexts Try utilizing new words in a variety of contexts, such as academic chats, everyday conversations, and formal writing.

input: Ask your professors, peers, or mentors for input on how you might improve your use of new vocabulary. You can improve your language abilities by receiving feedback that is constructive.

create a personal notebook or blog in which you actively utilize and investigate new language. Whether you choose to keep a journal or create a blog, the important thing is that you do it. Writing is an efficient method for you to hone your language talents as well as display them to others.

Practice Questions and Answers Explanations 2023-2024

Question 1 (Verbal):

Which of the following words is the antonym of "magnify"?

A) Decrease
B) Enlarge
C) Amplify
D) Expand

Answer and Explanation:

A) Decrease is the antonym of "magnify," as it means to make something smaller.

Question 2 (Reading):

In the passage, the author uses the term "equivocate" to suggest that the politician:

A) Was straightforward in his statements.
B) Used vague and ambiguous language.
C) Was an experienced debater.
D) Believed in honesty and transparency.

Answer and Explanation:
2) B) The author uses "equivocate" to indicate that the politician used vague and ambiguous language, avoiding clear statements.

Question 3 (Quantitative):

If x + 3 = 8, what is the value of x?

A) 4
B) 5
C) 6
D) 7

Answer and Explanation:
3) B) To find the value of x, subtract 3 from both sides of the equation: x + 3 - 3 = 8 - 3, which simplifies to x = 5.

Question 4 (Writing Sample):

Write a persuasive essay on the topic of the importance of environmental conservation. Support your argument with specific examples.

Answer and Explanation:
4) The answer should be a well-structured persuasive essay that discusses the importance of environmental conservation and provides examples to support the argument. The content of the essay may vary, so no specific answer is provided.

Question 5 (Verbal):

What is the synonym of "ephemeral"?

A) Eternal
B) Temporary
C) Endless
D) Permanent

Answer and Explanation:
5) B) "Ephemeral" means temporary or short-lived, making "temporary" a synonym.

Question 6 (Reading):

In the passage, what is the primary purpose of the author's use of the anecdote about the lost puppy?

A) To highlight the dangers of stray animals.
B) To emphasize the need for stricter pet ownership laws.
C) To engage the reader's emotions and support the argument.
D) To provide evidence of the author's personal experience.

Answer and Explanation:

6) C) The author uses the anecdote about the lost puppy to engage the reader's emotions and support the argument about the importance of responsible pet ownership.

Question 7 (Quantitative):

If a book costs $20 and is on sale for 25% off, what is the sale price of the book?

A) $5
B) $10
C) $15
D) $20

Answer and Explanation:
7) B) To find the sale price, multiply the original price by the discount percentage: $20 × 25% = $20 × 0.25 = $5. Subtract this discount from the original price: $20 - $5 = $15.

Question 8 (Writing Sample):

Write a letter to your school principal proposing a new recycling program. Explain the benefits of the program and how it can be implemented.

Answer and Explanation:
8) The answer should be a well-structured letter proposing a new recycling program, explaining its benefits, and providing details on its implementation. The content of the letter may vary, so no specific answer is provided.

Question 9 (Verbal):

Choose the word that is the antonym of "diligent."

A) Lazy
B) Hardworking
C) Industrious
D) Energetic

Answer and Explanation:
9) A) "Diligent" means hardworking or industrious, so the antonym is "lazy."

Question 10 (Reading):

What is the main idea of the passage?

A) The benefits of a healthy lifestyle.
B) The history of medical breakthroughs.
C) The importance of regular exercise.
D) The link between diet and overall health.

Answer and Explanation:
10) D) The main idea of the passage is the link between diet and overall health.

Question 11 (Quantitative):

If $3x = 15$, what is the value of x?

A) 5
B) 10
C) 15
D) 20

Answer and Explanation:
11) A) To find the value of x, divide both sides of the equation by 3: $3x/3 = 15/3$, which simplifies to $x = 5$.

Question 12 (Writing Sample):

Write a creative story about a young explorer's journey through a mysterious forest. Include vivid descriptions and unexpected discoveries.

Answer and Explanation:
12) The answer should be a creative story about a young explorer's journey through a mysterious forest, featuring vivid descriptions and unexpected discoveries. The content of the story may vary, so no specific answer is provided.

Question 13 (Verbal):

What is the synonym of "benevolent"?

A) Malevolent
B) Kind-hearted
C) Hostile
D) Mysterious

Answer and Explanation:
13) B) "Benevolent" means kind-hearted, making "kind-hearted" a synonym.

Question 14 (Reading):

In the passage, what is the author's attitude toward technology?

A) Enthusiastic
B) Indifferent
C) Critical
D) Uncertain

Answer and Explanation:
14) C) The author's attitude toward technology is critical, as indicated by concerns about its impact on human interactions.

Question 15 (Quantitative):

If a rectangle has a length of 8 units and a width of 6 units, what is the area of the rectangle?

A) 14 square units
B) 20 square units
C) 30 square units
D) 48 square units

Answer and Explanation:
15) D) To find the area of a rectangle, multiply its length by its width: 8 units × 6 units = 48 square units.

Question 16 (Writing Sample):

Write an argumentative essay on the topic of the impact of social media on interpersonal relationships. Provide evidence and examples to support your argument.

Answer and Explanation:
16) The answer should be a well-structured argumentative essay discussing the impact of social media on interpersonal relationships, supported by evidence and examples. The content of the essay may vary, so no specific answer is provided.

Question 17 (Verbal):

What is the antonym of "indignant"?

A) Angry
B) Delighted
C) Furious
D) Furious

Answer and Explanation:
17) B) The antonym of "indignant" is "delighted," as it represents a positive emotional state.

Question 18 (Reading):

In the passage, what is the central theme or message conveyed by the author?

A) The importance of teamwork in sports.
B) The history of a famous sports rivalry.
C) The value of sportsmanship and respect.
D) The competitive nature of professional athletes.

Answer and Explanation:
18) C) The central theme or message conveyed by the author is the value of sportsmanship and respect.

Question 19 (Quantitative):

If 2/3 of a number is 12, what is the number?

A) 8
B) 18
C) 16
D) 9

Answer and Explanation:
19) B) To find the number, you can set up an equation: (2/3)x = 12. Then, multiply both sides by 3/2 to solve for x: (3/2) * (2/3)x = (3/2) * 12. This simplifies to x = 18.

Question 20 (Writing Sample):

Write a persuasive essay on the topic of the importance of physical education in schools. Provide reasons and examples to support your argument.

Answer and Explanation:
20) The answer should be a well-structured persuasive essay discussing the importance of physical education in schools, supported by reasons and examples. The content of the essay may vary, so no specific answer is provided.

Question 21 (Verbal):

Which of the following words is the antonym of "superfluous"?

A) Necessary
B) Redundant
C) Excessive
D) Vital

Answer and Explanation:
21) A) "Superfluous" means unnecessary or excessive, so the antonym is "necessary."

Question 22 (Reading):

In the passage, the term "analogous" is used to compare two concepts. What does "analogous" mean in this context?

A) Different and unrelated
B) Similar or equivalent
C) Contradictory
D) Inconsequential

Answer and Explanation:
22) B) In this context, "analogous" means similar or equivalent, indicating that the two concepts share similarities.

Question 23 (Quantitative):

If a store offers a 20% discount on a $60 item, what is the sale price of the item?

A) $10
B) $12
C) $30
D) $48

Answer and Explanation:
23) C) To find the sale price, calculate the discount amount (20% of $60) and subtract it from the original price: $60 - (0.20 * $60) = $60 - $12 = $48.

Question 24 (Writing Sample):

Write an informative essay on the topic of the impact of climate change on ecosystems. Provide scientific evidence and examples to support your analysis.

Answer and Explanation:
24) The answer should be a well-structured informative essay discussing the impact of climate change on ecosystems, supported by scientific evidence and examples. The content of the essay may vary, so no specific answer is provided.

Question 25 (Verbal):

What is the synonym of "concur"?

A) Disagree
B) Differ
C) Agree
D) Contradict

Answer and Explanation:
25) C) "Concur" means to agree or be in harmony, so the synonym is "agree."

Question 26 (Reading):

In the passage, what does the author suggest about the effects of regular exercise on mental health?

A) Exercise has no impact on mental well-being.
B) Exercise can alleviate symptoms of depression and anxiety.
C) Exercise only benefits physical health.
D) The effects of exercise on mental health are unknown.

Answer and Explanation:
26) B) The author suggests that regular exercise can alleviate symptoms of depression and anxiety, indicating a positive impact on mental health.

Question 27 (Verbal):

Which of the following words is the antonym of "frugal"?

A) Wasteful
B) Thrifty
C) Economical
D) Stingy

Answer and Explanation:
27) A) "Frugal" means careful with money, so the antonym is "wasteful."

Question 28 (Reading):

In the passage, what is the primary message conveyed by the author?

A) The importance of embracing diversity.
B) The history of a cultural festival.
C) The impact of technology on traditions.
D) The decline of traditional customs.

Answer and Explanation:
28) C) The primary message conveyed by the author is the impact of technology on traditions.

Question 29 (Quantitative):

If 4/5 of a pizza has 8 slices, how many slices are there in the whole pizza?

A) 5
B) 10
C) 12
D) 16

Answer and Explanation:
29) B) To find the number of slices in the whole pizza, you can set up a proportion: (4/5) = 8/x. Cross-multiply to solve for x: 4x = 5 * 8, which simplifies to x = 10.

Question 30 (Writing Sample):

Write a descriptive essay about your favorite place in nature. Use vivid details to paint a picture of the place for your reader.

Answer and Explanation:
30) The answer should be a well-structured descriptive essay about the writer's favorite place in nature, using vivid details to create a sensory experience for the reader. The content of the essay may vary, so no specific answer is provided.

Question 31 (Verbal):

What is the synonym of "vivid"?

A) Faint
B) Lively
C) Dull
D) Obscure

Answer and Explanation:
31) B) "Vivid" means lively or full of life, making "lively" a synonym.

Question 32 (Reading):

In the passage, the term "allegory" is used to describe the story within a story. What does "allegory" mean in this context?

A) A symbolic narrative with a hidden meaning.
B) A story with a straightforward plot.
C) A fictional tale of adventure.
D) An historical account.

Answer and Explanation:
32) A) In this context, "allegory" means a symbolic narrative with a hidden meaning, indicating that the story within a story has a deeper significance.

Question 33 (Quantitative):

If the perimeter of a square is 16 inches, what is the length of one side of the square?

A) 2 inches
B) 4 inches
C) 6 inches
D) 8 inches

Answer and Explanation:
33) B) To find the length of one side of the square, divide the perimeter by 4 (since a square has four equal sides): 16 inches ÷ 4 = 4 inches.

Question 34 (Writing Sample):

Write an argumentative essay on the topic of the impact of social media on youth development. Provide evidence and examples to support your argument.

Answer and Explanation:
34) The answer should be a well-structured argumentative essay discussing the impact of social media on youth development, supported by evidence and examples. The content of the essay may vary, so no specific answer is provided.

Question 35 (Verbal):

What is the antonym of "proficient"?

A) Skilled
B) Inexperienced
C) Competent
D) Expert

Answer and Explanation:
35) B) The antonym of "proficient" is "inexperienced," indicating a lack of skill or expertise.

Question 36 (Reading):

What is the author's tone in the passage?

A) Objective
B) Sarcastic
C) Enthusiastic
D) Critical

Answer and Explanation:
36) C) The author's tone in the passage is enthusiastic, expressing excitement and positivity.

Question 37 (Quantitative):

If 3 dozen apples cost $18, how much does each apple cost?

A) $0.25
B) $0.50
C) $1.50
D) $6.00

Answer and Explanation:
37) B) To find the cost of each apple, divide the total cost by the number of apples: $18 ÷ 36 apples (3 dozen) = $0.50 per apple.

Question 38 (Writing Sample):

Write an informative essay on the topic of the impact of pollution on urban environments. Provide facts and examples to support your analysis.

Answer and Explanation:
38) The answer should be a well-structured informative essay discussing the impact of pollution on urban environments, supported by facts and examples. The content of the essay may vary, so no specific answer is provided.

Question 39 (Verbal):

What is the synonym of "incessant"?

A) Occasional
B) Relentless
C) Temporary
D) Intermittent

Answer and Explanation:
39) B) "Incessant" means relentless or continuous, making "relentless" a synonym.

Question 40 (Reading):

In the passage, what is the author's purpose in describing the character's internal struggle?

A) To create suspense in the narrative.
B) To provide background information about the character.
C) To develop the character's motivations and conflicts.
D) To introduce a new plot twist.

Answer and Explanation:
40) C) The author's purpose in describing the character's internal struggle is to develop the character's motivations and conflicts, adding depth to the narrative.

Question 41 (Quantitative):

If a car travels at a constant speed of 60 miles per hour, how many miles will it travel in 2.5 hours?

A) 120 miles
B) 150 miles
C) 125 miles
D) 100 miles

Answer and Explanation:
41) B) To find the distance traveled, multiply the speed by the time: 60 miles per hour × 2.5 hours = 150 miles.

Question 42 (Writing Sample):

Write a narrative essay about a memorable family vacation. Share the experiences, challenges, and joys you encountered during the trip.

Answer and Explanation:
42) The answer should be a well-structured narrative essay about a memorable family vacation, sharing experiences, challenges, and joys encountered during the trip. The content of the essay may vary, so no specific answer is provided.

Question 43 (Verbal):

What is the antonym of "exuberant"?

A) Energetic
B) Lively
C) Reserved
D) Excited

Answer and Explanation:
43) C) The antonym of "exuberant" is "reserved," indicating a more restrained or quiet demeanor.

Question 44 (Reading):

In the passage, the term "metaphor" is used to describe the author's comparison of the city to a living organism. What does "metaphor" mean in this context?

A) A literal description of a city.
B) A direct comparison between two unlike things.
C) An abstract concept.
D) An historical account.

Answer and Explanation:
44) B) In this context, "metaphor" means a direct comparison between two unlike things, as the author compares the city to a living organism for illustrative purposes.

Question 45 (Quantitative):

If a box contains 24 candies, and you take out 3 candies, what fraction of the candies remains in the box?

A) 1/6
B) 1/8
C) 7/8
D) 3/8

Answer and Explanation:

45) D) To find the fraction that remains, subtract the number of candies taken out from the total number of candies: (24 - 3)/24 = 21/24, which simplifies to 7/8.

Question 46 (Writing Sample):

Write a persuasive essay on the importance of volunteer work in the community. Provide reasons and examples to support your argument.

Answer and Explanation:
46) The answer should be a well-structured persuasive essay discussing the importance of volunteer work in the community, supported by reasons and examples. The content of the essay may vary, so no specific answer is provided.

Question 47 (Verbal):

What is the synonym of "ephemeral"?

A) Permanent
B) Eternal
C) Transitory
D) Timeless

Answer and Explanation:
47) C) "Ephemeral" means transitory or lasting for a very short time, making "transitory" a synonym.

Question 48 (Reading):

In the passage, the author's tone can best be described as:

A) Objective
B) Humorous
C) Biased
D) Indifferent

Answer and Explanation:
48) A) The author's tone in the passage is objective, as it presents information without expressing a particular emotional stance.

Question 49 (Quantitative):

If a toy costs $18 and is on sale for 30% off, what is the sale price of the toy?

A) $5.40
B) $12.60
C) $5.60
D) $18.30

Answer and Explanation:
49) B) To find the sale price, calculate the discount amount (30% of $18) and subtract it from the original price: $18 - (0.30 * $18) = $18 - $5.40 = $12.60.

Question 50 (Writing Sample):

Write a descriptive essay about a remarkable person in your life. Describe their qualities and the impact they've had on you.

Answer and Explanation:
50) The answer should be a well-structured descriptive essay about a remarkable person in the writer's life, describing their qualities and the impact they've had. The content of the essay may vary, so no specific answer is provided.

Question 51 (Verbal):

What is the antonym of "superfluous"?

A) Necessary
B) Redundant
C) Excessive
D) Vital

Answer and Explanation:
51) A) "Superfluous" means unnecessary or excessive, so the antonym is "necessary."

Question 52 (Reading):

In the passage, what does the author imply about the main character's future?

A) The character will face numerous challenges.
B) The character will achieve great success.
C) The character's future is uncertain.
D) The character will remain content with the status quo.

Answer and Explanation:
52) C) The author implies that the character's future is uncertain, suggesting an element of unpredictability.

Question 53 (Quantitative):

If 5/6 of a book has 180 pages, how many pages are there in the entire book?

A) 108 pages
B) 216 pages
C) 150 pages
D) 120 pages

Answer and Explanation:
53) B) To find the number of pages in the entire book, you can set up a proportion: (5/6) = 180/x. Cross-multiply to solve for x: 5x = 6 * 180, which simplifies to x = 216 pages.

Question 54 (Writing Sample):

Write an argumentative essay on the topic of the impact of video games on children's development. Provide evidence and examples to support your argument.

Answer and Explanation:
54) The answer should be a well-structured argumentative essay discussing the impact of video games on children's development, supported by evidence and examples. The content of the essay may vary, so no specific answer is provided.

Question 55 (Verbal):

What is the synonym of "vivid"?

A) Faint
B) Lively
C) Dull
D) Obscure

Answer and Explanation:
55) B) "Vivid" means lively or full of life, making "lively" a synonym.

Question 56 (Reading):

In the passage, the author's tone can best be described as:

A) Objective
B) Sarcastic
C) Enthusiastic
D) Critical

Answer and Explanation:
56) C) The author's tone in the passage is enthusiastic, expressing excitement and positivity.

Question 57 (Quantitative):

If a box contains 36 marbles, and 1/4 of the marbles are red, how many marbles are red?

A) 6
B) 9
C) 18
D) 12

Answer and Explanation:
57) B) To find the number of red marbles, multiply the total number of marbles by 1/4: (1/4) * 36 = 9 red marbles.

Question 58 (Writing Sample):

Write an informative essay on the topic of the impact of technology on education. Provide statistics and real-world examples to support your analysis.

Answer and Explanation:
58) The answer should be a well-structured informative essay discussing the impact of technology on education, supported by statistics and real-world examples. The content of the essay may vary, so no specific answer is provided.

Question 59 (Verbal):

What is the antonym of "meritorious"?

A) Deserving
B) Blameworthy
C) Praiseworthy
D) Commendable

Answer and Explanation:
59) B) The antonym of "meritorious" is "blameworthy," indicating actions or behavior deserving blame.

Question 60 (Reading):

In the passage, the author uses the term "allegory" to describe the symbolic elements in the story. What does "allegory" mean in this context?

A) A straightforward narrative.
B) A hidden message or symbolic representation.
C) A humorous tale.
D) An ancient legend.

Answer and Explanation:
60) B) In this context, "allegory" means a hidden message or symbolic representation, suggesting that the story contains deeper meanings.

Question 61 (Quantitative):

If a bicycle travels at a speed of 15 miles per hour and is ridden for 2.5 hours, how far will it have traveled?

A) 25 miles
B) 30 miles
C) 35 miles
D) 37.5 miles

Answer and Explanation:
61) B) To find the distance traveled, multiply the speed by the time: 15 miles per hour × 2.5 hours = 30 miles.

Question 62 (Writing Sample):

Write a persuasive essay on the importance of cultural diversity in schools. Provide reasons and examples to support your argument.

Answer and Explanation:
62) The answer should be a well-structured persuasive essay discussing the importance of cultural diversity in schools, supported by reasons and examples. The content of the essay may vary, so no specific answer is provided.

Question 63 (Verbal):

What is the synonym of "ephemeral"?

A) Eternal
B) Temporary
C) Endless
D) Permanent

Answer and Explanation:
63) B) "Ephemeral" means temporary or short-lived, making "temporary" a synonym.

Question 64 (Reading):

In the passage, the author's tone can best be described as:

A) Objective
B) Sarcastic
C) Enthusiastic
D) Critical

Answer and Explanation:
64) D) The author's tone in the passage is critical, expressing disapproval or concern.

Question 65 (Quantitative):

If a textbook costs $40, and the price is reduced by 20%, what is the sale price of the textbook?

A) $32
B) $8
C) $48
D) $10

Answer and Explanation:
65) A) To find the sale price, calculate the discount amount (20% of $40) and subtract it from the original price: $40 - (0.20 * $40) = $40 - $8 = $32.

Question 66 (Writing Sample):

Write an informative essay on the topic of the impact of deforestation on wildlife and ecosystems. Provide scientific evidence and examples to support your analysis.

Answer and Explanation:
66) The answer should be a well-structured informative essay discussing the impact of deforestation on wildlife and ecosystems, supported by scientific evidence and examples. The content of the essay may vary, so no specific answer is provided.

Question 67 (Verbal):

What is the antonym of "proficient"?

A) Skilled
B) Inexperienced
C) Competent
D) Expert

Answer and Explanation:
67) B) The antonym of "proficient" is "inexperienced," indicating a lack of skill or expertise.

Question 68 (Reading):

In the passage, what is the author's attitude toward modern technology?

A) Enthusiastic
B) Indifferent
C) Critical
D) Uncertain

Answer and Explanation:
68) C) The author's attitude toward modern technology is critical, as indicated by concerns about its impact on society.

Question 69 (Quantitative):

If a box contains 48 pencils, and 1/3 of the pencils are red, how many pencils are red?

A) 8
B) 16
C) 12
D) 24

Answer and Explanation:
69) B) To find the number of red pencils, multiply the total number of pencils by 1/3: (1/3) * 48 = 16 red pencils.

Question 70 (Writing Sample):

Write a persuasive essay on the benefits of a balanced diet and regular exercise. Provide reasons and examples to support your argument.

Answer and Explanation:
70) The answer should be a well-structured persuasive essay discussing the benefits of a balanced diet and regular exercise, supported by reasons and examples. The content of the essay may vary, so no specific answer is provided.

Question 71 (Verbal):

What is the synonym of "vivid"?

A) Faint
B) Lively
C) Dull
D) Obscure

Answer and Explanation:
71) B) "Vivid" means lively or full of life, making "lively" a synonym.

Question 72 (Reading):

In the passage, the author's tone can best be described as:

A) Objective
B) Sarcastic
C) Enthusiastic
D) Critical

Answer and Explanation:
72) A) The author's tone in the passage is objective, presenting information without expressing a particular emotional stance.

Question 73 (Quantitative):

If a computer is sold at a 15% discount and its original price is $800, what is the sale price of the computer?

A) $680
B) $720
C) $7200
D) $760

Answer and Explanation:
73) A) To find the sale price, calculate the discount amount (15% of $800) and subtract it from the original price: $800 - (0.15 * $800) = $800 - $120 = $680.

Question 74 (Writing Sample):

Write an argumentative essay on the impact of social media on privacy. Provide evidence and examples to support your argument.

Answer and Explanation:
74) The answer should be a well-structured argumentative essay discussing the impact of social media on privacy, supported by evidence and examples. The content of the essay may vary, so no specific answer is provided.

Question 75 (Verbal):

What is the antonym of "superfluous"?

A) Necessary
B) Redundant
C) Excessive
D) Vital

Answer and Explanation:
75) A) "Superfluous" means unnecessary or excessive, so the antonym is "necessary."

Question 76 (Reading):

In the passage, the author's attitude toward the main character can best be described as:

A) Objective
B) Sympathetic
C) Critical
D) Indifferent

Answer and Explanation:
76) B) The author's attitude toward the main character is sympathetic, indicating a sense of understanding and compassion.

Question 77 (Quantitative):

If a bicycle travels at a speed of 12 kilometers per hour and is ridden for 3 hours, how far will it have traveled?

A) 30 kilometers
B) 36 kilometers
C) 48 kilometers
D) 72 kilometers

Answer and Explanation:
77) B) To find the distance traveled, multiply the speed by the time: 12 kilometers per hour × 3 hours = 36 kilometers.

Question 78 (Writing Sample):

Write an informative essay on the topic of the impact of climate change on agriculture. Provide scientific evidence and examples to support your analysis.

Answer and Explanation:
78) The answer should be a well-structured informative essay discussing the impact of climate change on agriculture, supported by scientific evidence and examples. The content of the essay may vary, so no specific answer is provided.

Question 79 (Verbal):

What is the synonym of "ephemeral"?

A) Eternal
B) Temporary
C) Endless
D) Permanent

Answer and Explanation:
79) B) "Ephemeral" means temporary or short-lived, making "temporary" a synonym.

Question 80 (Reading):

In the passage, the author's tone can best be described as:

A) Objective
B) Humorous
C) Biased
D) Indifferent

Answer and Explanation:
80) A) The author's tone in the passage is objective, presenting information without expressing a particular emotional stance.

Question 81 (Verbal):

What is the antonym of "proficient"?

A) Skilled
B) Inexperienced
C) Competent
D) Expert

Answer and Explanation:
81) B) The antonym of "proficient" is "inexperienced," indicating a lack of skill or expertise.

Question 82 (Reading):

In the passage, what is the author's attitude toward the main character?

A) Objective
B) Sympathetic
C) Critical
D) Indifferent

Answer and Explanation:
82) B) The author's attitude toward the main character is sympathetic, indicating a sense of understanding and compassion.

Question 83 (Quantitative):

If a bicycle travels at a speed of 12 kilometers per hour and is ridden for 2.5 hours, how far will it have traveled?

A) 24 kilometers
B) 30 kilometers
C) 36 kilometers
D) 48 kilometers

Answer and Explanation:
83) C) To find the distance traveled, multiply the speed by the time: 12 kilometers per hour × 2.5 hours = 30 kilometers.

Question 84 (Writing Sample):

Write a persuasive essay on the benefits of recycling. Provide reasons and examples to support your argument.

Answer and Explanation:
84) The answer should be a well-structured persuasive essay discussing the benefits of recycling, supported by reasons and examples. The content of the essay may vary, so no specific answer is provided.

Question 85 (Verbal):

What is the synonym of "vivid"?

A) Faint
B) Lively
C) Dull
D) Obscure

Answer and Explanation:
85) B) "Vivid" means lively or full of life, making "lively" a synonym.

Question 86 (Reading):

In the passage, the author's tone can best be described as:

A) Objective
B) Humorous
C) Biased
D) Indifferent

Answer and Explanation:
86) A) The author's tone in the passage is objective, presenting information without expressing a particular emotional stance.

Question 87 (Quantitative):

If a computer is sold at a 20% discount and its original price is $1,200, what is the sale price of the computer?

A) $900
B) $960
C) $1,080
D) $1,140

Answer and Explanation:
87) B) To find the sale price, calculate the discount amount (20% of $1,200) and subtract it from the original price: $1,200 - (0.20 * $1,200) = $1,200 - $240 = $960.

Question 88 (Writing Sample):

Write an informative essay on the topic of the impact of pollution on marine life. Provide scientific evidence and examples to support your analysis.

Answer and Explanation:
88) The answer should be a well-structured informative essay discussing the impact of pollution on marine life, supported by scientific evidence and examples. The content of the essay may vary, so no specific answer is provided.

Question 89 (Verbal):

What is the antonym of "superfluous"?

A) Necessary
B) Redundant
C) Excessive
D) Vital

Answer and Explanation:
89) A) "Superfluous" means unnecessary or excessive, so the antonym is "necessary."

Question 90 (Reading):

In the passage, the author's tone can best be described as:

A) Objective
B) Sarcastic
C) Enthusiastic
D) Critical

Answer and Explanation:
90) B) The author's tone in the passage is sarcastic, using humor to express criticism.

Question 91 (Quantitative):

If a box contains 60 candies, and 1/5 of the candies are blue, how many candies are blue?

A) 6
B) 10
C) 12
D) 15

Answer and Explanation:
91) D) To find the number of blue candies, multiply the total number of candies by 1/5: (1/5) * 60 = 15 blue candies.

Question 92 (Writing Sample):

Write a persuasive essay on the importance of renewable energy sources. Provide reasons and examples to support your argument.

Answer and Explanation:
92) The answer should be a well-structured persuasive essay discussing the importance of renewable energy sources, supported by reasons and examples. The content of the essay may vary, so no specific answer is provided.

Question 93 (Verbal):

What is the synonym of "ephemeral"?

A) Eternal
B) Temporary
C) Endless
D) Permanent

Answer and Explanation:
93) B) "Ephemeral" means temporary or short-lived, making "temporary" a synonym.

Question 94 (Reading):

In the passage, the author's attitude toward the main character can best be described as:

A) Objective
B) Sympathetic
C) Critical
D) Indifferent

Answer and Explanation:
94) C) The author's attitude toward the main character is critical, expressing disapproval or concern.

Question 95 (Quantitative):

If a box contains 36 marbles, and 1/6 of the marbles are green, how many marbles are green?

A) 6
B) 12
C) 18
D) 24

Answer and Explanation:
95) B) To find the number of green marbles, multiply the total number of marbles by 1/6: (1/6) * 36 = 12 green marbles.

Question 96 (Writing Sample):

Write an informative essay on the topic of the impact of deforestation on climate change. Provide scientific evidence and examples to support your analysis.

Answer and Explanation:
96) The answer should be a well-structured informative essay discussing the impact of deforestation on climate change, supported by scientific evidence and examples. The content of the essay may vary, so no specific answer is provided.

Question 97 (Verbal):

What is the antonym of "meritorious"?

A) Deserving
B) Blameworthy
C) Praiseworthy
D) Commendable

Answer and Explanation:
97) B) The antonym of "meritorious" is "blameworthy," indicating actions or behavior deserving blame.

Question 98 (Reading):

In the passage, the author's tone can best be described as:

A) Objective
B) Humorous
C) Biased
D) Indifferent

Answer and Explanation:
98) A) The author's tone in the passage is objective, presenting information without expressing a particular emotional stance.

Question 99 (Quantitative):

If a car travels at a constant speed of 50 miles per hour and is driven for 4 hours, how far will it have traveled?

A) 100 miles
B) 150 miles
C) 200 miles
D) 250 miles

Answer and Explanation:
99) C) To find the distance traveled, multiply the speed by the time: 50 miles per hour × 4 hours = 200 miles.

Question 100 (Writing Sample):

Write a persuasive essay on the importance of community service. Provide reasons and examples to support your argument.

Answer and Explanation:
100) The answer should be a well-structured persuasive essay discussing the importance of community service, supported by reasons and examples. The content of the essay may vary, so no specific answer is provided.

Question 101 (Verbal):

What is the synonym of "vivid"?

A) Faint
B) Lively
C) Dull
D) Obscure

Answer and Explanation:
101) B) "Vivid" means lively or full of life, making "lively" a synonym.

Question 102 (Reading):

In the passage, the author's tone can best be described as:

A) Objective
B) Sarcastic
C) Enthusiastic
D) Critical

Answer and Explanation:
102) C) The author's tone in the passage is enthusiastic, expressing excitement and positivity.

Question 103 (Quantitative):

If a bicycle travels at a speed of 18 kilometers per hour and is ridden for 3 hours, how far will it have traveled?

A) 36 kilometers
B) 54 kilometers
C) 72 kilometers
D) 108 kilometers

Answer and Explanation:
103) B) To find the distance traveled, multiply the speed by the time: 18 kilometers per hour × 3 hours = 54 kilometers.

Question 104 (Writing Sample):

Write an informative essay on the topic of the impact of technology on personal relationships. Provide real-life examples to support your analysis.

Answer and Explanation:
104) The answer should be a well-structured informative essay discussing the impact of technology on personal relationships, supported by real-life examples. The content of the essay may vary, so no specific answer is provided.

Question 105 (Verbal):

What is the antonym of "superfluous"?

A) Necessary
B) Redundant
C) Excessive
D) Vital

Answer and Explanation:
105) A) "Superfluous" means unnecessary or excessive, so the antonym is "necessary."

Question 106 (Reading):

In the passage, the author's attitude toward modern technology can best be described as:

A) Enthusiastic
B) Indifferent
C) Critical
D) Uncertain

Answer and Explanation:
106) C) The author's attitude toward modern technology is critical, as indicated by concerns about its impact on society.

Question 107 (Quantitative):

If a box contains 72 pencils, and 1/4 of the pencils are blue, how many pencils are blue?

A) 6
B) 12
C) 18
D) 24

Answer and Explanation:
107) B) To find the number of blue pencils, multiply the total number of pencils by 1/4: (1/4) * 72 = 18 blue pencils.

Question 108 (Writing Sample):

Write a persuasive essay on the benefits of a well-balanced education that includes both arts and sciences. Provide reasons and examples to support your argument.

Answer and Explanation:
108) The answer should be a well-structured persuasive essay discussing the benefits of a well-balanced education that includes both arts and sciences, supported by reasons and examples. The content of the essay may vary, so no specific answer is provided.

Question 109 (Verbal):

What is the synonym of "ephemeral"?

A) Eternal
B) Temporary
C) Endless
D) Permanent

Answer and Explanation:
109) B) "Ephemeral" means temporary or short-lived, making "temporary" a synonym.

Question 110 (Reading):

In the passage, the author's attitude toward the main character can best be described as:

A) Objective
B) Sympathetic
C) Critical
D) Indifferent

Answer and Explanation:
110) C) The author's attitude toward the main character is critical, expressing disapproval or concern.

Question 111 (Quantitative):

If a bicycle travels at a speed of 15 miles per hour and is ridden for 2 hours, how far will it have traveled?

A) 15 miles
B) 20 miles
C) 30 miles
D) 40 miles

Answer and Explanation:
111) C) To find the distance traveled, multiply the speed by the time: 15 miles per hour × 2 hours = 30 miles.

Question 112 (Writing Sample):

Write an informative essay on the topic of the impact of social media on mental health. Provide statistics and real-life examples to support your analysis.

Answer and Explanation:
112) The answer should be a well-structured informative essay discussing the impact of social media on mental health, supported by statistics and real-life examples. The content of the essay may vary, so no specific answer is provided.

Question 113 (Verbal):

What is the antonym of "meritorious"?

A) Deserving
B) Blameworthy
C) Praiseworthy
D) Commendable

Answer and Explanation:
113) B) The antonym of "meritorious" is "blameworthy," indicating actions or behavior deserving blame.

Question 114 (Reading):

In the passage, the author's tone can best be described as:

A) Objective
B) Humorous
C) Biased
D) Indifferent

Answer and Explanation:
114) A) The author's tone in the passage is objective, presenting information without expressing a particular emotional stance.

Question 115 (Quantitative):

If a box contains 80 candies, and 1/8 of the candies are green, how many candies are green?

A) 5
B) 10
C) 15
D) 20

Answer and Explanation:
115) B) To find the number of green candies, multiply the total number of candies by 1/8: (1/8) * 80 = 10 green candies.

Question 116 (Writing Sample):

Write a persuasive essay on the importance of a healthy work-life balance. Provide reasons and examples to support your argument.

Answer and Explanation:
116) The answer should be a well-structured persuasive essay discussing the importance of a healthy work-life balance, supported by reasons and examples. The content of the essay may vary, so no specific answer is provided.

Question 117 (Verbal):

What is the synonym of "vivid"?

A) Faint
B) Lively
C) Dull
D) Obscure

Answer and Explanation:
117) B) "Vivid" means lively or full of life, making "lively" a synonym.

Question 118 (Reading):

In the passage, the author's tone can best be described as:

A) Objective
B) Sarcastic
C) Enthusiastic
D) Critical

Answer and Explanation:
118) A) The author's tone in the passage is objective, presenting information without expressing a particular emotional stance.

Question 119 (Quantitative):

If a computer is sold at a 25% discount and its original price is $1,500, what is the sale price of the computer?

A) $375
B) $1,125
C) $1,375
D) $1,475

Answer and Explanation:
119) B) To find the sale price, calculate the discount amount (25% of $1,500) and subtract it from the original price: $1,500 - (0.25 * $1,500) = $1,500 - $375 = $1,125.

Question 120 (Writing Sample):

Write an informative essay on the topic of the impact of climate change on sea levels. Provide scientific evidence and examples to support your analysis.

Answer and Explanation:
120) The answer should be a well-structured informative essay discussing the impact of climate change on sea levels, supported by scientific evidence and examples. The content of the essay may vary, so no specific answer is provided.

Question 121 (Verbal):

What is the antonym of "superfluous"?

A) Necessary
B) Redundant
C) Excessive
D) Vital

Answer and Explanation:
121) A) "Superfluous" means unnecessary or excessive, so the antonym is "necessary."

Question 122 (Reading):

In the passage, the author's attitude toward modern technology can best be described as:

A) Enthusiastic
B) Indifferent
C) Critical
D) Uncertain

Answer and Explanation:
122) C) The author's attitude toward modern technology is critical, as indicated by concerns about its impact on society.

Question 123 (Quantitative):

If a box contains 90 pencils, and 1/9 of the pencils are blue, how many pencils are blue?

A) 6
B) 10
C) 15
D) 20

Answer and Explanation:
123) B) To find the number of blue pencils, multiply the total number of pencils by 1/9: (1/9) * 90 = 10 blue pencils.

Question 124 (Writing Sample):

Write a persuasive essay on the importance of empathy in interpersonal relationships. Provide reasons and examples to support your argument.

Answer and Explanation:
124) The answer should be a well-structured persuasive essay discussing the importance of empathy in interpersonal relationships, supported by reasons and examples. The content of the essay may vary, so no specific answer is provided.

Question 125 (Verbal):

What is the synonym of "ephemeral"?

A) Eternal
B) Temporary
C) Endless
D) Permanent

Answer and Explanation:
125) B) "Ephemeral" means temporary or short-lived, making "temporary" a synonym.

Question 126 (Reading):

In the passage, the author's attitude toward the main character can best be described as:

A) Objective
B) Sympathetic
C) Critical
D) Indifferent

Answer and Explanation:
126) C) The author's attitude toward the main character is critical, expressing disapproval or concern.

Question 127 (Quantitative):

If a bicycle travels at a speed of 20 kilometers per hour and is ridden for 2.5 hours, how far will it have traveled?

A) 25 kilometers
B) 40 kilometers
C) 50 kilometers
D) 60 kilometers

Answer and Explanation:
127) C) To find the distance traveled, multiply the speed by the time: 20 kilometers per hour × 2.5 hours = 50 kilometers.

Question 128 (Writing Sample):

Write an informative essay on the topic of the impact of social media on society's perception of beauty. Provide real-life examples to support your analysis.

Answer and Explanation:
128) The answer should be a well-structured informative essay discussing the impact of social media on society's perception of beauty, supported by real-life examples. The content of the essay may vary, so no specific answer is provided.

Question 129 (Verbal):

What is the antonym of "meritorious"?

A) Deserving
B) Blameworthy
C) Praiseworthy
D) Commendable

Answer and Explanation:
129) B) The antonym of "meritorious" is "blameworthy," indicating actions or behavior deserving blame.

Question 130 (Reading):

In the passage, the author's tone can best be described as:

A) Objective
B) Humorous
C) Biased
D) Indifferent

Answer and Explanation:
130) A) The author's tone in the passage is objective, presenting information without expressing a particular emotional stance.

Question 131 (Verbal):

What is the synonym of "luminous"?

A) Dark
B) Bright
C) Faint
D) Obscure

Answer and Explanation:
131) B) "Luminous" means bright or emitting light, making "bright" a synonym.

Question 132 (Reading):

In the passage, the author's attitude toward the main character can best be described as:

A) Objective
B) Sympathetic
C) Critical
D) Indifferent

Answer and Explanation:
132) A) The author's attitude toward the main character is objective, presenting information without expressing a particular emotional stance.

Question 133 (Quantitative):

If a car travels at a constant speed of 60 miles per hour and is driven for 2 hours, how far will it have traveled?

A) 60 miles
B) 120 miles
C) 180 miles
D) 240 miles

Answer and Explanation:
133) B) To find the distance traveled, multiply the speed by the time: 60 miles per hour × 2 hours = 120 miles.

Question 134 (Writing Sample):

Write a persuasive essay on the benefits of extracurricular activities in schools. Provide reasons and examples to support your argument.

Answer and Explanation:
134) The answer should be a well-structured persuasive essay discussing the benefits of extracurricular activities in schools, supported by reasons and examples. The content of the essay may vary, so no specific answer is provided.

Question 135 (Verbal):

What is the antonym of "volatile"?

A) Stable
B) Unpredictable
C) Changeable
D) Inconsistent

Answer and Explanation:
135) A) The antonym of "volatile" is "stable," indicating a lack of rapid or unpredictable changes.

Question 136 (Reading):

In the passage, the author's tone can best be described as:

A) Objective
B) Sarcastic
C) Enthusiastic
D) Critical

Answer and Explanation:
136) D) The author's tone in the passage is critical, expressing disapproval or concern.

Question 137 (Quantitative):

If a box contains 96 marbles, and 1/6 of the marbles are green, how many marbles are green?

A) 12
B) 16
C) 18
D) 24

Answer and Explanation:
137) B) To find the number of green marbles, multiply the total number of marbles by 1/6: (1/6) * 96 = 16 green marbles.

Question 138 (Writing Sample):

Write an informative essay on the topic of the impact of air pollution on human health. Provide scientific evidence and examples to support your analysis.

Answer and Explanation:
138) The answer should be a well-structured informative essay discussing the impact of air pollution on human health, supported by scientific evidence and examples. The content of the essay may vary, so no specific answer is provided.

Question 139 (Verbal):

What is the synonym of "ephemeral"?

A) Eternal
B) Temporary
C) Endless
D) Permanent

Answer and Explanation:
139) B) "Ephemeral" means temporary or short-lived, making "temporary" a synonym.

Question 140 (Reading):

In the passage, the author's attitude toward modern technology can best be described as:

A) Enthusiastic
B) Indifferent
C) Critical
D) Uncertain

Answer and Explanation:
140) A) The author's attitude toward modern technology is enthusiastic, expressing excitement and positivity.

Question 141 (Quantitative):

If a car is sold at a 15% discount and its original price is $25,000, what is the sale price of the car?

A) $2,500
B) $21,250
C) $22,500
D) $23,750

Answer and Explanation:

141) B) To find the sale price, calculate the discount amount (15% of $25,000) and subtract it from the original price: $25,000 - (0.15 * $25,000) = $25,000 - $3,750 = $21,250.

Question 142 (Writing Sample):

Write a persuasive essay on the importance of cultural diversity in the workplace. Provide reasons and examples to support your argument.

Answer and Explanation:
142) The answer should be a well-structured persuasive essay discussing the importance of cultural diversity in the workplace, supported by reasons and examples. The content of the essay may vary, so no specific answer is provided.

Question 143 (Verbal):

What is the antonym of "meritorious"?

A) Deserving
B) Blameworthy
C) Praiseworthy
D) Commendable

Answer and Explanation:
143) B) The antonym of "meritorious" is "blameworthy," indicating actions or behavior deserving blame.

Question 144 (Reading):

In the passage, the author's tone can best be described as:

A) Objective
B) Humorous
C) Biased
D) Indifferent

Answer and Explanation:
144) A) The author's tone in the passage is objective, presenting information without expressing a particular emotional stance.

Question 145 (Quantitative):

If a box contains 120 candies, and 1/10 of the candies are blue, how many candies are blue?

A) 6
B) 12
C) 18
D) 24

Answer and Explanation:
145) B) To find the number of blue candies, multiply the total number of candies by 1/10: (1/10) * 120 = 12 blue candies.

Question 146 (Writing Sample):

Write an informative essay on the topic of the impact of technology on education. Provide real-life examples to support your analysis.

Answer and Explanation:
146) The answer should be a well-structured informative essay discussing the impact of technology on education, supported by real-life examples. The content of the essay may vary, so no specific answer is provided.

Question 147 (Verbal):

What is the synonym of "ephemeral"?

A) Eternal
B) Temporary
C) Endless
D) Permanent

Answer and Explanation:
147) B) "Ephemeral" means temporary or short-lived, making "temporary" a synonym.

Question 148 (Reading):

In the passage, the author's attitude toward the main character can best be described as:

A) Objective
B) Sympathetic
C) Critical
D) Indifferent

Answer and Explanation:
148) C) The author's attitude toward the main character is critical, expressing disapproval or concern.

Question 149 (Quantitative):

If a car travels at a constant speed of 65 miles per hour and is driven for 3 hours, how far will it have traveled?

A) 65 miles
B) 130 miles
C) 195 miles
D) 260 miles

Answer and Explanation:
149) C) To find the distance traveled, multiply the speed by the time: 65 miles per hour × 3 hours = 195 miles.

Question 150 (Writing Sample):

Write a persuasive essay on the benefits of reading for pleasure. Provide reasons and examples to support your argument.

Answer and Explanation:
150) The answer should be a well-structured persuasive essay discussing the benefits of reading for pleasure, supported by reasons and examples. The content of the essay may vary, so no specific answer is provided.

Question 151 (Verbal):

What is the antonym of "volatile"?

A) Stable
B) Unpredictable
C) Changeable
D) Inconsistent

Answer and Explanation:
151) A) The antonym of "volatile" is "stable," indicating a lack of rapid or unpredictable changes.

Question 152 (Reading):

In the passage, the author's tone can best be described as:

A) Objective
B) Sarcastic
C) Enthusiastic
D) Critical

Answer and Explanation:
152) B) The author's tone in the passage is sarcastic, using humor to express criticism.

Question 153 (Quantitative):

If a box contains 144 marbles, and 1/12 of the marbles are green, how many marbles are green?

A) 8
B) 12
C) 16
D) 24

Answer and Explanation:
153) B) To find the number of green marbles, multiply the total number of marbles by 1/12: (1/12) * 144 = 12 green marbles.

Question 154 (Writing Sample):

Write an informative essay on the topic of the impact of video games on cognitive development. Provide research findings and examples to support your analysis.

Answer and Explanation:
154) The answer should be a well-structured informative essay discussing the impact of video games on cognitive development, supported by research findings and examples. The content of the essay may vary, so no specific answer is provided.

Question 155 (Verbal):

What is the synonym of "luminous"?

A) Dark
B) Bright
C) Faint
D) Obscure

Answer and Explanation:
155) B) "Luminous" means bright or emitting light, making "bright" a synonym.

Question 156 (Reading):

In the passage, the author's attitude toward modern technology can best be described as:

A) Enthusiastic
B) Indifferent
C) Critical
D) Uncertain

Answer and Explanation:
156) C) The author's attitude toward modern technology is critical, as indicated by concerns about its impact on society.

Question 157 (Quantitative):

If a car is sold at a 30% discount and its original price is $30,000, what is the sale price of the car?

A) $6,000
B) $21,000
C) $24,000
D) $27,000

Answer and Explanation:
157) B) To find the sale price, calculate the discount amount (30% of $30,000) and subtract it from the original price: $30,000 - (0.30 * $30,000) = $30,000 - $9,000 = $21,000.

Question 158 (Writing Sample):

Write a persuasive essay on the importance of physical fitness in maintaining overall health. Provide reasons and examples to support your argument.

Answer and Explanation:
158) The answer should be a well-structured persuasive essay discussing the importance of physical fitness in maintaining overall health, supported by reasons and examples. The content of the essay may vary, so no specific answer is provided.

Question 159 (Verbal):

What is the synonym of "ephemeral"?

A) Eternal
B) Temporary
C) Endless
D) Permanent

Answer and Explanation:
159) B) "Ephemeral" means temporary or short-lived, making "temporary" a synonym.

Question 160 (Reading):

In the passage, the author's attitude toward the main character can best be described as:

A) Objective
B) Sympathetic
C) Critical
D) Indifferent

Answer and Explanation:
160) B) The author's attitude toward the main character is sympathetic, indicating a sense of understanding and compassion.

Question 161 (Quantitative):

If a car travels at a constant speed of 70 miles per hour and is driven for 4 hours, how far will it have traveled?

A) 70 miles
B) 140 miles
C) 280 miles
D) 350 miles

Answer and Explanation:
161) C) To find the distance traveled, multiply the speed by the time: 70 miles per hour × 4 hours = 280 miles.

Question 162 (Writing Sample):

Write an informative essay on the topic of the impact of social media on political discourse. Provide real-life examples to support your analysis.

Answer and Explanation:
162) The answer should be a well-structured informative essay discussing the impact of social media on political discourse, supported by real-life examples. The content of the essay may vary, so no specific answer is provided.

Question 163 (Verbal):

What is the antonym of "volatile"?

A) Stable
B) Unpredictable
C) Changeable
D) Inconsistent

Answer and Explanation:
163) A) The antonym of "volatile" is "stable," indicating a lack of rapid or unpredictable changes.

Question 164 (Reading):

In the passage, the author's tone can best be described as:

A) Objective
B) Sarcastic
C) Enthusiastic
D) Critical

Answer and Explanation:
164) A) The author's tone in the passage is objective, presenting information without expressing a particular emotional stance.

Question 165 (Quantitative):

If a box contains 180 candies, and 1/15 of the candies are green, how many candies are green?

A) 9
B) 12
C) 15
D) 18

Answer and Explanation:
165) B) To find the number of green candies, multiply the total number of candies by 1/15: (1/15) * 180 = 12 green candies.

Question 166 (Writing Sample):

Write a persuasive essay on the importance of arts education in schools. Provide reasons and examples to support your argument.

Answer and Explanation:
166) The answer should be a well-structured persuasive essay discussing the importance of arts education in schools, supported by reasons and examples. The content of the essay may vary, so no specific answer is provided.

Question 167 (Verbal):

What is the synonym of "luminous"?

A) Dark
B) Bright
C) Faint
D) Obscure

Answer and Explanation:
167) B) "Luminous" means bright or emitting light, making "bright" a synonym.

Question 168 (Reading):

In the passage, the author's attitude toward modern technology can best be described as:

A) Enthusiastic
B) Indifferent
C) Critical
D) Uncertain

Answer and Explanation:
168) C) The author's attitude toward modern technology is critical, as indicated by concerns about its impact on society.

Question 169 (Quantitative):

If a car is sold at a 20% discount and its original price is $35,000, what is the sale price of the car?

A) $5,000
B) $21,000
C) $28,000
D) $33,000

Answer and Explanation:
169) B) To find the sale price, calculate the discount amount (20% of $35,000) and subtract it from the original price: $35,000 - (0.20 * $35,000) = $35,000 - $7,000 = $28,000.

Question 170 (Writing Sample):

Write a persuasive essay on the importance of renewable energy sources in combating climate change. Provide reasons and examples to support your argument.

Answer and Explanation:
170) The answer should be a well-structured persuasive essay discussing the importance of renewable energy sources in combating climate change, supported by reasons and examples. The content of the essay may vary, so no specific answer is provided.

Question 171 (Verbal):

What is the synonym of "ephemeral"?

A) Eternal
B) Temporary
C) Endless
D) Permanent

Answer and Explanation:
171) B) "Ephemeral" means temporary or short-lived, making "temporary" a synonym.

Question 172 (Reading):

In the passage, the author's attitude toward the main character can best be described as:

A) Objective
B) Sympathetic
C) Critical
D) Indifferent

Answer and Explanation:
172) D) The author's attitude toward the main character is indifferent, indicating a lack of emotional attachment or concern.

Question 173 (Quantitative):

If a car travels at a constant speed of 75 miles per hour and is driven for 5 hours, how far will it have traveled?

A) 75 miles
B) 150 miles
C) 375 miles
D) 500 miles

Answer and Explanation:
173) D) To find the distance traveled, multiply the speed by the time: 75 miles per hour × 5 hours = 375 miles.

Question 174 (Writing Sample):

Write an informative essay on the topic of the impact of deforestation on biodiversity. Provide scientific evidence and examples to support your analysis.

Answer and Explanation:
174) The answer should be a well-structured informative essay discussing the impact of deforestation on biodiversity, supported by scientific evidence and examples. The content of the essay may vary, so no specific answer is provided.

Question 175 (Verbal):

What is the antonym of "volatile"?

A) Stable
B) Unpredictable
C) Changeable
D) Inconsistent

Answer and Explanation:
175) A) The antonym of "volatile" is "stable," indicating a lack of rapid or unpredictable changes.

Question 176 (Reading):

In the passage, the author's tone can best be described as:

A) Objective
B) Sarcastic
C) Enthusiastic
D) Critical

Answer and Explanation:
176) D) The author's tone in the passage is critical, expressing disapproval or concern.

Question 177 (Quantitative):

If a box contains 200 marbles, and 1/20 of the marbles are green, how many marbles are green?

A) 10
B) 20
C) 30
D) 40

Answer and Explanation:
177) B) To find the number of green marbles, multiply the total number of marbles by 1/20: (1/20) * 200 = 20 green marbles.

Question 178 (Writing Sample):

Write a persuasive essay on the importance of empathy in resolving conflicts. Provide reasons and examples to support your argument.

Answer and Explanation:
178) The answer should be a well-structured persuasive essay discussing the importance of empathy in resolving conflicts, supported by reasons and examples. The content of the essay may vary, so no specific answer is provided.

Question 179 (Verbal):

What is the synonym of "luminous"?

A) Dark
B) Bright
C) Faint
D) Obscure

Answer and Explanation:
179) B) "Luminous" means bright or emitting light, making "bright" a synonym.

Question 180 (Reading):

In the passage, the author's attitude toward modern technology can best be described as:

A) Enthusiastic
B) Indifferent
C) Critical
D) Uncertain

Answer and Explanation:
180) C) The author's attitude toward modern technology is critical, as indicated by concerns about its impact on society.

Question 181 (Verbal):

What is the antonym of "ubiquitous"?

A) Rare
B) Common
C) Pervasive
D) Widespread

Answer and Explanation:
181) A) "Ubiquitous" means present everywhere, so the antonym is "rare."

Question 182 (Reading):

In the passage, the author's attitude toward the main character can best be described as:

A) Objective
B) Sympathetic
C) Critical
D) Indifferent

Answer and Explanation:
182) B) The author's attitude toward the main character is sympathetic, indicating a sense of understanding and compassion.

Question 183 (Quantitative):

If a box contains 220 candies, and 1/22 of the candies are blue, how many candies are blue?

A) 10
B) 20
C) 30
D) 40

Answer and Explanation:
183) B) To find the number of blue candies, multiply the total number of candies by 1/22: (1/22) * 220 = 20 blue candies.

Question 184 (Writing Sample):

Write a persuasive essay on the importance of reducing single-use plastics. Provide reasons and examples to support your argument.

Answer and Explanation:
184) The answer should be a well-structured persuasive essay discussing the importance of reducing single-use plastics, supported by reasons and examples. The content of the essay may vary, so no specific answer is provided.

Question 185 (Verbal):

What is the synonym of "ephemeral"?

A) Eternal
B) Temporary
C) Endless
D) Permanent

Answer and Explanation:
185) B) "Ephemeral" means temporary or short-lived, making "temporary" a synonym.

Question 186 (Reading):

In the passage, the author's tone can best be described as:

A) Objective
B) Sarcastic
C) Enthusiastic
D) Critical

Answer and Explanation:
186) A) The author's tone in the passage is objective, presenting information without expressing a particular emotional stance.

Question 187 (Quantitative):

If a car is sold at a 10% discount and its original price is $45,000, what is the sale price of the car?

A) $4,500
B) $36,000
C) $40,500
D) $45,500

Answer and Explanation:
187) B) To find the sale price, calculate the discount amount (10% of $45,000) and subtract it from the original price: $45,000 - (0.10 * $45,000) = $45,000 - $4,500 = $36,000.

Question 188 (Writing Sample):

Write an informative essay on the topic of the impact of music on emotional well-being. Provide scientific evidence and examples to support your analysis.

Answer and Explanation:
188) The answer should be a well-structured informative essay discussing the impact of music on emotional well-being, supported by scientific evidence and examples. The content of the essay may vary, so no specific answer is provided.

Question 189 (Verbal):

What is the antonym of "volatile"?

A) Stable
B) Unpredictable
C) Changeable
D) Inconsistent

Answer and Explanation:
189) A) The antonym of "volatile" is "stable," indicating a lack of rapid or unpredictable changes.

Question 190 (Reading):

In the passage, the author's attitude toward modern technology can best be described as:

A) Enthusiastic
B) Indifferent
C) Critical
D) Uncertain

Answer and Explanation:
190) D) The author's attitude toward modern technology is uncertain, as indicated by a lack of clear enthusiasm or criticism.

Question 191 (Quantitative):

If a box contains 240 marbles, and 1/24 of the marbles are green, how many marbles are green?

A) 10
B) 20
C) 30
D) 40

Answer and Explanation:
191) B) To find the number of green marbles, multiply the total number of marbles by 1/24: (1/24) * 240 = 20 green marbles.

Question 192 (Writing Sample):

Write a persuasive essay on the importance of physical exercise in maintaining a healthy lifestyle. Provide reasons and examples to support your argument.

Answer and Explanation:
192) The answer should be a well-structured persuasive essay discussing the importance of physical exercise in maintaining a healthy lifestyle, supported by reasons and examples. The content of the essay may vary, so no specific answer is provided.

Question 193 (Verbal):

What is the synonym of "luminous"?

A) Dark
B) Bright
C) Faint
D) Obscure

Answer and Explanation:
193) B) "Luminous" means bright or emitting light, making "bright" a synonym.

Question 194 (Reading):

In the passage, the author's attitude toward the main character can best be described as:

A) Objective
B) Sympathetic
C) Critical
D) Indifferent

Answer and Explanation:
194) C) The author's attitude toward the main character is critical, expressing disapproval or concern.

Question 195 (Quantitative):

If a car travels at a constant speed of 80 miles per hour and is driven for 6 hours, how far will it have traveled?

A) 80 miles
B) 160 miles
C) 320 miles
D) 480 miles

Answer and Explanation:
195) D) To find the distance traveled, multiply the speed by the time: 80 miles per hour × 6 hours = 480 miles.

Question 196 (Writing Sample):

Write an informative essay on the topic of the impact of climate change on wildlife habitats. Provide scientific evidence and examples to support your analysis.

Answer and Explanation:
196) The answer should be a well-structured informative essay discussing the impact of climate change on wildlife habitats, supported by scientific evidence and examples. The content of the essay may vary, so no specific answer is provided.

Question 197 (Verbal):

What is the antonym of "ubiquitous"?

A) Rare
B) Common
C) Pervasive
D) Widespread

Answer and Explanation:
197) A) "Ubiquitous" means present everywhere, so the antonym is "rare."

Question 198 (Reading):

In the passage, the author's tone can best be described as:

A) Objective
B) Sarcastic
C) Enthusiastic
D) Critical

Answer and Explanation:
198) A) The author's tone in the passage is objective, presenting information without expressing a particular emotional stance.

Question 199 (Quantitative):

If a box contains 260 candies, and 1/26 of the candies are blue, how many candies are blue?

A) 10
B) 20
C) 30
D) 40

Answer and Explanation:
199) B) To find the number of blue candies, multiply the total number of candies by 1/26: (1/26) * 260 = 20 blue candies.

Question 200 (Writing Sample):

Write a persuasive essay on the importance of biodiversity conservation. Provide reasons and examples to support your argument.

Answer and Explanation:
200) The answer should be a well-structured persuasive essay discussing the importance of biodiversity conservation, supported by reasons and examples. The content of the essay may vary, so no specific answer is provided.

Made in United States
Troutdale, OR
11/20/2023